The Passion of Jerome

'Breathtaking . . . there's enough in the brilliant development of his drama to suggest that the vitality of Irish theatrical language is safe in his hands.' *The Guardian*

'The relentless honesty of his writing is savage and refreshing.' *Time Out*

'A far-from-ordinary imagination.' *The Observer*

Dermot Bolger was born in Finglas, North Dublin, in 1959, and has worked as a factory hand, library assistant and publisher. His debut play *The Lament for Arthur Cleary* (1989) received The Samuel Beckett Award for best first play in Britain, The Stewart Parker BBC Prize and an Edinburgh Festival Fringe First Award. Other works include two 1990 one-act plays – *In High Germany* (later filmed by RTE television) and *The Holy Ground* (for which he received his second Edinburgh Fringe First Award), both staged by the Gate Theatre in Dublin. *The Passion of Jerome* is his fourth play to be staged by the Abbey Theatre in Dublin on their Peacock stage – following on from *Blinded by the Light* (1990), *One Last White Horse* (1991) and *April Bright* (1995). In 1985 he published his first novel, *Night Shift* (which received the AE Memorial Prize) and followed it in 1987 with *The Woman's Daughter* (for which he received the Macaulay Fellowship). He has since published four other novels, *The Journey Home* (1990), *Emily's Shoes* (1992), *A Second Life* (1994) – all published, like his first two novels, by Penguin – and *Father's Music* (Flamingo, 1997). He is the author of six volumes of poetry, the most recent being *Taking My Letters Back – New & Selected Poems* (New Island Books, 1998). In 1997 he devised and edited the best-selling collaborative novel, *Finbar's Hotel* – which he co-wrote along with six other Irish novelists, and followed it in 1999 with *Finbar's Hotel II: Ladies Night*. He has edited many other books, including *The Picador Book of Contemporary Irish Fiction*. Between 1977 and 1992 he founded and r̴ polemic Raven Arts Press in Dub

T0262478

The Passion of Jerome

BY DERMOT BOLGER

Methuen Drama

For Nick Marston

A Methuen Drama Modern Play

Published by Methuen Drama

2 4 6 8 10 9 7 5 3 1

Copyright © 1999 by Dermot Bolger

Dermot Bolger has asserted his right under the Copyright, Designs and Patents Act, 1988 to be identified as the author of this work.

The author would like to gratefully acknowledge Anglo-Irish Bank's sponsorship of the position of Playwright in Association in the Abbey Theatre, Ciara and Roddy, and Temple Bar Properties who provided a writer's studio in which a draft of this play was completed.

First published in the United Kingdom in 1999 by Methuen Publishing Limited,

Peribo Pty Ltd, 58 Beaumont Road, Mount Kuring-Gai NSW 2080, Australia, ACN 002 273761 (for Australia and New Zealand)

A CIP catalogue record for this book is available from the British Library

ISBN 0 413 73880 9

New Island edition (To be sold in Ireland only) ISBN 1 902602 05 6

Typeset by MATS, Southend-on-Sea, Essex

Caution

THE PASSION OF JEROME

Dermot Bolger

The Passion of Jerome by Dermot Bolger was written in 1997 whilst he was Anglo Irish Bank Writer-In-Association at the Abbey Theatre. The production was first staged in the Peacock Theatre, Dublin on 11th February 1999. Press Night was 17th February 1999. The cast, in order of appearance was

Jerome Liam Carney **Clara** Lisa Harding **Derek** Ronan Leahy **Penny** Donna Dent **Priest** Des Nealon **Caretaker** Johnny Murphy **Rita** Máire Ní Ghráinne **Doctor** Barry Barnes **Thugs** Des Fleming, Kieran Kenny and Ronan Leahy

Director David Byrne **Designer** Monica Frawley **Lighting Designer** Trevor Dawson

Foreword

What would WB Yeats, who conceived of the notion of an Irish Literary Theatre a hundred years ago this year, have made of Irish drama today? Inherited in the 1980s and '90s by a third wave of dramatists, Irish drama has never before been written in such abundance, or been in such demand nationally and internationally from managements, audiences, publishers and academics.

The landscape out of which it is being written would surely have astonished him. A tentative description, as yet unforseeable, has very recently entered the political vocabulary here: 'the new Ireland'. Light years away from colonial repression and deference, this 'new Ireland' is already young, educated, self possessed and increasingly secular. Unhampered by Yeats' patriotism and nationalism, it is a fully signed up member of the European Union. Free from Joyce's fretting in the shadows of mother tongue and coloniser's tongue, it is also computer literate and adept at information technology. Prospering from the aggressive 'Celtic Tiger' economy, this is also the day of the entrepreneur and of duty free hedonism. In short, cultural unease seems to have gone forever and Irish art in all its forms, though particularly theatre, is in international demand. As the century closes, Irish culture is chic.

It is impossible to know what Yeats would have made of 'the new Ireland' as it is to generalise about its new drama. Two impulses, though, seem to characterise it. There are those playwrights who revel in and express the cultural DNA of the times, in all its pluralisms and vertiginous newness. And there are those who, Janus like, also look back and indeed write back to a time before Yeats, back to the seanachai, and the Greeks before them. Dermot Bolger's The Passion of Jerome belongs to the second category: unchic and radical in that its subject matter is the sacred phenomenon of the stigmata. Bolger's play directly addresses Celtic Tiger Dublin and, in affinity with Yeats, casts a cold eye. Therefore, it seems entirely appropriate that, a hundred years on in Yeats' theatre, this play should be the first in a new series of National Theatre programme playscript publications. My thanks to both Methuen and New Island publications and, above all, to Dermot Bolger for making this exciting development possible.

Patrick Mason, Artistic Director, The Abbey Theatre

Dermot Bolger

Born in Finglas, North Dublin, in 1959, Dermot Bolger has worked as a factory hand, library assistant and publisher. His debut play, **The Lament for Arthur Cleary** (1989), received The Samuel Beckett Award (for B[est] First Play in Britain), The Stewart Parker BBC Prize and an Edinburgh Festival Fringe First Award. Other works include two 1990 one-act plays - **In High Germany** (later filmed by RTE television) and **The Holy Ground** (for which he received his second Edinburgh Fringe First Award), both staged by the Gate Theatre[,] Dublin. **The Passion of Jerome** is his fourth play to be staged by the Abbey Theatre in Dublin on its Peaco[ck] stage - following on from **Blinded by the Light** (1990), **One Last White Horse** (1991) and **April Bright** (1995)[.] 1985 he published his first novel, **Night Shift** (which received the AE Memorial Prize) and followed it in 19[8?] with **The Woman's Daughter** (for which he received the Macualay Fellowship). He has since published fo[ur] other novels, **The Journey Home** (1990), **Emily's Shoes** (1992), **A Second Life** (1994) - all published, like hi[s] first two novels, by Penguin and **Father's Music** (Flamingo, 1997). He is the author of six volumes of poetr[y] the most recent being **Taking My Letters Back - New & Selected Poems** (New Island Books, 1998). In 1997 he devised and edited the best-selling collaborative novel, **Finbar's Hotel** - which he co-wrote along with other Irish novelists, and followed it in 1999 with **Finbar's Hotel II: Ladies Night**. He has edited many othe[r] books, including **The Picador Book of Contemporary Irish Fiction** and between 1977 and 1992 he founded and ran the Raven Arts Press in Dublin.

David Byrne

David studied under Frank Dermody and Tomás MacAnna at the Abbey Theatre's National School of Dram[a] and has worked extensively with both the Abbey Company and at the Gate Theatre with the Edwards/ MacLiammoir Company. In 1975 he joined Radio Telefís Eireann, this brought him into the area of Young People's programming where he worked as Writer/Producer. A founder member of Wet Paint Arts and Artistic Director since its inception in 1984, he wrote and directed six works, winning in 1985 the Arts Council's Experimental Theatre Award. In 1988 he first began working with Dermot Bolger, this culminate[d] in the 1989 Dublin Theatre Festival production of Dermot's **The Lament for Arthur Cleary, Tramway End** (Gate Theatre), **One Last White Horse** (Peacock Theatre) and **April Bright** at the Peacock. He is the winne[r] of a number of national and international awards including a Fringe First in the 1990 and again in the 199[?] Edinburgh Festival. In 1991 he was appointed New Writing Editor at the Abbey Theatre under Artistic Director Garry Hynes where he developed and directed **Ullaloo**, a new play by Marina Carr, **The Winter Th[ief]** by Sean MacMathuna and Jimmy Murphy's **Brothers of the Brush** which won the Irish Life Award in the 19[?] Dublin Theatre Festival and in 1997 he directed **A Picture of Paradise** also by Jimmy Murphy at the Peaco[ck] Theatre. He has collaborated with John Waters on **Easter Dues** for Bickerstaffe Theatre following on from their previous award-winning **Long Black Coat**.

Monica Frawley

An honours graduate of Central/St Martins School of Art and Design, Monica has worked with all the maj[or] theatre companies in Ireland. Her work has been seen in Britain, the United States, France, Canada and Australia. Her recent work includes **Juno and the Paycock** for the Abbey Theatre, **Mutabilitie** by Frank McGuinness for the Royal National Theatre, London and Marina Carr's **By the Bog of Cats** for the Abbey Theatre

Trevor Dawson

Trevor Dawson is from Sheffield, Yorkshire. He began his career in stage management and then moved to Belfast, where he lived for ten years, working as a production manager and lighting designer for the Lyric Theatre. Lighting design for the Abbey Theatre includes **The Silver Dollar Boys, You Can't Take It With You, The Silver Tassle, Dancing At Lughnasa, Faith Healer, The Plough And The Stars, Conversations On A Homecoming, Moving, Purple Dust, The Cuchulain Cycle, Masks Of Transformation, Sacred Mysteries, Strange Occurrence On Ireland's Eye, A Crucial Week In The Life Of A Grocer's Assistant, The Trojan Women[,] The Cavalcaders, The Bird Sanctuary, The Well Of The Saints, April Bright, Sour Grapes, Juno and the Paycock, At Swim-Two-Birds** and **The Rivals**. He has lit over fifty shows for the Lyric company including **Equus, The Seagull, A Midsummer Night's Dream, Mary Stuart, The Mikado** and **Northern Star**. In Dublin he has designed the lighting for **How The Other Half Loves** at the Olympia; **A Christmas Carol, A Woman Of No Importance, Arrah-Na-Pogue, The Recruiting Officer, Uncle Vanya, The Importance Of Being Earnest, The Rivals, Absurd Person Singular** and **Salome** at the Gate. Trevor is production manager at the Abbey Theatre.

Amharclann Na Mainistreach
The National Theatre Society Limited

Board
John Fanning
Bernard Farrell
James Hickey
(Chairman)
Gemma Hussey
Jennifer Johnston
Niall O'Brien
Deirdre Purcell
Conor Skehan
Tony Wakefield

Artistic Director
Patrick Mason

Managing Director
Richard Wakely

Company Secretary/General Manager
Martin Fahy

Executive P.A.
Marie Kelly

Literary Manager
Judy Friel

Dramaturg
Aideen Howard

Literary Assistant
Caroline Dennehy

Archivist
Mairead Delaney

Voice Coach
Andrea Ainsworth

Associate Directors
Brian Brady
Conall Morrison

Staff Director
Jason Byrne

Outreach Director
Kathy McArdle

Education Officer
Sharon Murphy

Projects and Office Manager
Jean O'Dwyer

Abbey Players
Kathleen Barrington
Jane Brennan
Desmond Cave
Fedelma Cullen
Clive Geraghty
Maire Ni Ghrainne
Brid Ni Neachtain
Niall O'Brien
Macdara O Fatharta
Maire O'Neill

Head of PR and Marketing
Madeline Boughton

Promotions Officer
Gilly Clarke

Press Assistant
Lucy McKeever

Box Office Manager
Adam Lawlor

Box Office Assistant
Des Byrne

Box Office Clerks
Clare Downey
Gretchen Frieman
Karen Hynes
Martha Keaney
Anne Marie Ryan
Lisa Murray
Cliona McNamara

House Manager
Pauline Morrison

Front of House
Carmel Bamwell
John Baynes
Ruth Colgen
Con Doyle
Ivan Kavanagh
Ann Marie Mulvey
Seamus Mallin
Jim O'Keeffe
John Rooney
William Redmond
Lee Smith
Sandra Williams
David Windrim

Accountant
Margaret Bradley

Accounts
Margaret Flynn

Payroll
Pat O'Connell

Receptionists
Celina Carey
Yvonne Murphy

Production Manager
Trevor Dawson

Production Coordinator
Karen Weavers

Production Assistant
Vanessa Fitz-Simon

Scenic Artists
Angie Benner
Jonathan Garrett
Jennifer Moonan

Property Master
Stephen Molloy

Wardrobe Supervisor
Anne Cave

Deputy
Joan O'Clery
Vickie Miller
Anne O' Mahony
Fiona Talbot

Lighting Supervisor
Tony Wakefield

Deputy
Mick Doyle
Michael Wright
Alan Wakefield

Sound
Dave Nolan
Dave O'Brien
Nuala Golden

Master Carpenter
Peter Rose

Deputy
Mark Darley

Carpenters
John Kavanagh
Al Carroll

Stage Managers
John Andrews
Gerry Doyle

Stage Hands
Aaron Clear
Mike Doyle
Pat Dillon

Stage Door Keepers
Patrick Gannon
Patrick Whelan

Stage Directors
Head of Department
Finola Eustace

Colette Morris
John Stapleton

Assistant Stage Managers
Catriona Behan
Stephen Dempsey
Brendan McLoughlin

Maintenance Engineer
Brian Fennell

Assistant
Tony Delaney

Cleaning Supervisor
Joe McNamara

Shareholders
The Minister for Arts Heritage, Gaeltacht and the Islands
The Minister for Finance
Robert Ballagh
Kathleen Barrington
Sebastian Barry
Marina Carr
Des Cave
Frank Clarke
Monica Corcoran
Fedelma Cullen
Gerald Dawe
Joe Dowling
Eugene Downes
Mick Doyle
Clare Duignan
John Fairleigh
Patrick Forde
Clive Geraghty
Des Geraghty
Maire Holmes
Michael Judge
Peadar Lamb
Mary Lennon
John Lynch
Tomas Mac Anna
Muriel McCarthy
Fiach MacConghail
Emer McNamara
Donal Nevin
Dave Nolan
Jim Nolan
Ulick O'Connor
Tony O'Dalaigh
Joan O'Hara
Mary O'Malley
Liam O'Maonlai
Peter Sheridan
Constance Short

Writer-in-Association
Thomas Kilroy
The position of Writer In-Association is sponsored by Anglo-Irish Bank

Honorary Associate Directors
Vincent Dowling
Tomás MacAnna

RTÉ
Supporting The Arts

The Arts Council
An Chomhairle Ealaíon

The Passion of Jerome

Characters

Jerome
Clara
Derek
Caretaker
Doctor
Penny
Rita
Priest
Down-and-out*
First Thug*
Second Thug*
Third Thug*

*It is preferable that the three thugs be played by young unmasked actors – one of whom (possibly **Third Thug** who has the least dialogue) may overlap and play the **Down-and-Out**. However, in smaller productions it may be possible for these thugs to be played in mask by the **Doctor** (**First Thug**), **Caretaker** (**Second Thug**) and **Priest** (**Third Thug** and possibly also overlapping as the **Down-and-Out**). The actress playing **Clara** – although we don't recognise her – should also play the role of a **Nurse** in Scene Three, Act Two.

Act One

Scene One

Just enough light bleeds into the darkness for us to discern a bed, back of centre stage, with a satin coverlet. A loose structure of stacked packing cases (some of which may be upturned so that items can be removed) has been created on three sides of the bed. A lamp rests on the case closest to the bed. These (along with paint cans, a book of wallpaper samples and other props) all suggest a limited moving into an empty flat, but they may also be used to create a loose sense of the very walls of the flat itself.

Now, as additional (although still indistinct) light rises we see **Clara** *(in her early twenties) on the bed with the coverlet wrapped like a cloak around her naked shoulders as she sits astride* **Jerome** *(who is approaching forty) to whom she is making love. They both writhe in the throes of sexual abandonment. The lighting begins to flicker, creating an even more haunting atmosphere as the coverlet falls from her naked back and she screams his name.*

Clara Jerome!

We hit an immediate blackout. Seconds pass before soft light comes up, as if a sheet of moonlight was lighting the room. They both lie curled beneath the sheets, voices relaxed and sleepy.

Clara (*softly*) You know something? You're the only man who's ever made me come like that.

Jerome Tonight was special. You always liked the hint of danger.

Clara (*reaching for her cigarettes beside the bed*) A room is just a room.

Jerome No. There's something sexual about this flat . . . stripped down, bare, circumcised.

Clara (*amused, lighting up*) I hope we never get a job writing estate agents' brochures.

Jerome   You know what I mean. You can even smell it, if you can smell anything over that smoke.

Clara   What?

Jerome   Animal lust. Rattling at the radiators, coursing through the walls. All the junkies and criminals squatting in the flats below us. Just think what they'd like to do to you.

Clara (*teasing laugh*)   Much the same things as you've just done . . . only better and for longer. Besides, who says the men in my life were all soft-bellied accountants?

Jerome   You're choosy in everything. You were never in Ballymun before in your life, even on safari.

A mobile phone by the bed begins to ring. Both look at it.

Jerome   Alex.

Clara   He's worried about the Silverskin presentation on Friday morning.

Jerome (*picking the phone up*)   That man will die of stress. (*Speaks into the phone in a put-on voice.*) 'The person you have dialled may be out of coverage or have their phone disconnected. Please try again later.' (*He flicks it off and tosses it down the bed.*) These tower blocks are only meant for fucking in. You couldn't live out here.

Clara   Thousands do. (*Reaches for the phone.*) Give me that, I want to call a taxi.

Jerome   Living is too big a word. They exist.

Clara (*leaning up on one elbow to dial*)   You can be an awful stuck-up bastard, you know that . . . especially for an uncircumcised bogman.

Jerome (*trying to take the phone from her*)   Being born in a stable doesn't make you a donkey.

Clara (*twisting around, amused, shielding the phone*)   It doesn't make you God Almighty either. Pride is a sin.

Jerome   It couldn't be. Pride exists.

Clara   Very clever. (*Speaks into the phone.*) Hello . . .

Jerome (*suddenly manages to snatch the phone and switch it off*)
Got ya! What's your hurry, Miss Nicotine?

Clara (*aiming a mock punch at him*)   I don't want to miss *ER* on
television. Now give it back here.

Jerome   No. I'm not like your accountants, all sensitive and
limp.

Clara   Do you think of anything except that cock of yours?

Jerome (*tossing the phone over her head into the corner*)   My cock is
perfectly capable of thinking for itself.

Clara   So I've noticed. (*She stubs out her cigarette.*) I don't know
which of you is getting more uppity.

Jerome (*pulls her on top of him*)   Well, at least here's your
chance to shut one of us up.

*She gasps for a moment as he thrusts into her, then grips his hair fiercely
with both hands.*

Clara   Bastard. I bet I can shut both of you up.

She kisses him violently as **Jerome** *begins to move beneath her under the
coverlet and lights fade. When the lights come back up* **Clara** *is sitting
on the edge of the bed in her bra and knickers, putting her blouse on. She
picks up the cigarette packet and moves away from the bed, doing her
buttons up.* **Jerome** *sleepily lies on in bed.*

Clara   Three times in one night. Is forty that terrifying?

Jerome   I'm trying to prove nothing to nobody.

Clara (*picking up her skirt*)   Not even yourself? I think I'll get a
twenty-three-year-old lover when I'm forty.

Jerome   Why?

Clara (*fastening her skirt on*)   Because twenty-three goes into
forty more often than the other way around.

Jerome   If I'd wanted a maths lesson I'd have picked
somebody with . . .

Clara   Bigger brains and smaller tits?

Jerome   You've brains to burn and you know it. You're going places.

Clara   I know. For the last hour I've been going home.

Jerome   Wait a while.

Clara   I don't need to prove something by doing it four times. And I'll not be responsible for your heart if you do. You've a wife to be responsible for that.

She stares at him, coolly lighting a cigarette.

Jerome   You've a cruel streak in you.

Clara (*blowing a smoke ring*)   We've that much in common so. What have you hidden this time?

Jerome   Don't go . . . not yet.

Clara   You always say that. (*Looking under the bed.*) If it's not my knickers, it's my shoes. (*She fishes one shoe out and puts it on.*) I had *ER* taping from experience but I'm not going to miss my Wednesday night dose of *Friends*.

She spots the other shoe and puts it on. She mimes glancing out of an invisible window. **Jerome** *sees her black horn-rimmed glasses on the packing case beside the bed and slips them under the pillow, then swings his feet out of the bed and stretches. He is naked except for a pair of boxer shorts.*

Clara   It is kind of exciting here. An incredible view! If this wasn't Ballymun these flats could change hands for quarter of a million.

Jerome   We could meet here for decades and no one would ever find us.

Clara *idly opens the wallpaper sample book and flicks through some of the pages.*

Clara   I had the Caribbean more in mind for illicit trysts, St Lucia.

Jerome   That's the problem with the Caribbean, you'll always meet somebody you sat beside in the National Concert Hall. Ballymun is Antarctica, shoals of shuffling penguins and a few mad scientists studying them.

Clara (*fingering one sample*)   You must be paying for Derek's wallpaper. This one is so thick he'll be peeling it off the wall to use as roach paper. Did he learn nothing from being busted?

Jerome   His brains got burnt along with the ancestors of the agricultural siblings they found on him. Give me concrete any day.

Clara *leaves the smoking cigarette down on the nearest packing case and reaches for her jacket.*

Clara   That's why you've such a big garden in Malahide, is it?

Jerome *glances into a shopping bag at his feet and produces a large carving knife. She is oblivious to him creeping towards her, holding the bag in his other hand.*

Jerome   It keeps Penny happy. If she gets overly fond of any vegetable I can chop it up with my cleaver like a jealous husband.

He suddenly slams the knife down on the packing case, slicing her cigarette in half. **Clara** *turns, startled.*

Jerome   Smoking after sex: it's overrated, damaging to your health and gives adultery a bad name.

Clara   I can look after my own health.

Jerome   I prefer something really sinful and indulgent . . . (*He roots in the shopping bag again to produce a lemon, which he tosses in the air, catches, then cuts in half with the knife.*) Earl Grey tea with real lemon.

Clara   God, I can't wait to be middle-aged.

Jerome   Penny and I couldn't do without our Earl Grey. (*Looks around.*) Where's the kettle? I told Derek I wouldn't babysit his flat unless he remembered to leave a kettle.

Clara   When's he going to England?

Jerome   In the morning. After he's bummed the boat fare and provided he and Catherine don't drink it first.

Clara   You're hard on him.

Jerome   'I'm sorry, Jerome, but your brother's a bum,' says Penny, one hundred per cent accurate, as she is about most things.

Clara (*starting to comb out her hair*)   Penny's nice. I feel I've made a good friend in her.

Jerome (*searching in a packing case*)   You didn't need to buy that watercolour. You couldn't afford it, certainly not on the wages we pay you.

Clara   I liked her colours . . . they're so innocent, blue-blooded primitive – Rathlin Island meets The Swiss Chalet Finishing School. (*Beat.*) Does she never suspect?

Jerome   People are happy with what they don't know. Leave her that way. Where's the blasted kettle?

Clara   I was hardly going to tell her. I just wondered.

Jerome (*stops and looks at her*)   She's the only person I ever loved.

Clara   That's rich.

Jerome   It's honest. I'm an honest hypocrite.

Clara   I never loved nothing, except my sleigh, Rosebud. Does she like me? Tell the truth.

Jerome (*rummaging in another case*)   She thinks you're good for me, some of your ambition may rub off and I'll start looking for design work again.

Clara   And will you?

He produces an ancient, battered electric kettle and stares at it in baffled wonder.

Jerome   Very chic. Dunne's Stores, Carlow, 1971. (*Looks* *up.*) That was Penny's dream marrying me. Her painting in her sunlit studio, with me upstairs at my drawing board, designing mould-breaking housing schemes for the poor.

Clara   As against composing jingles for cars and banks.

Jerome (*pulling on his trousers*)   We don't call them jingles in the trade. People hum tunes from ads, people who own kettles like this, the shuffling penguins out here. (*He exits into the wings, carrying the kettle.*) What chance the Corporation remembered to turn the water on?

In his absence **Clara** *deliberately lights up another cigarette and gleefully puffs as much smoke as possible around the bed.*

Clara   Since when did you care about ordinary people?

Jerome (*off-stage over the sound of running water*)   I stopped caring about architecture a long time ago too.

Clara   You mean you copped out, a serious lack of ambition.

Jerome *returns, holding the kettle that is obviously full. He kneels to try and plug it into a socket built into the floor.*

Jerome (*sniffing the smoke*)   It wouldn't happen to you. You'd fuck your way there, if needs be, and have a smoke afterwards.

Clara   It's a fuck or be fucked world. My glasses, they're missing.

She looks around for them, as **Jerome** *manages to almost hammer the plug into the socket. He rises, shadowing her movements.*

Jerome   I was too ambitious. The world doesn't need another second rate architect churning out warrens of apartments for tax break investors. It had to be cathedrals or burst for me, and no one builds cathedrals now except to shop in.

Clara   You've hidden my glasses, haven't you? (*She makes for the bed.*) At least Derek and Catherine have a bit of get up and go in them.

Jerome (*playfully blocking her path*)   I'll give them a week before their latest pipe dream evaporates. He's a dreamer, in the hands of a hard woman. Dad was the same, writing off pissed to *Opportunity Knocks* as Carlow's 'ivory-tinkling dentist'. Derek inherited his weaknesses.

Clara   And you got his strengths?

She makes a dive for the bed and **Jerome** *lands with her, pinning her wrists as she tries to reach under the pillow.*

Jerome   He didn't have any. Extracting teeth was a big step up for my Dad from being a printer. One year my mother got herself elected on to the light opera society committee, all of us brought out to a posh restaurant by the chairman and his wife. (*Again he restrains* **Clara**'s *hands from reaching under the pillow.*) The waiter brings a bottle of Chateau Plonk and the chairman waves towards my father. (*Posh voice.*) 'Perhaps my guest would honour us with his opinion.' The waiter holds out the bottle to Dad before he pours it. The poor man is totally baffled, then he whips out his reading glasses (**Jerome** *grabs* **Clara**'s *glasses from under the pillow and puts them on, miming his father's action.*) and peers at the label, before smiling at the waiter with the authority of generations of *Carlow Nationalist* printers: (*Father's voice.*) 'A first-rate printing job.'

Clara (*whipping the glasses off him and putting them on*)   You're making it up.

Jerome   I wish I was. Poor Da, married to a woman whose only two sisters were nuns. Every Christmas visit he'd ply the old hags with sherry and claim that he felt like a thorn surrounded by roses. (*Nun's voice.*) 'Well, you may feel like a thorn, Michael,' Sister Monica answers back one year, after downing her usual four glasses of sherry, 'but I've never felt your prick.'

Clara (*laughs*)   That one I don't believe.

Jerome   No, you're right. Me and Derek spent every Christmas dying for it to happen, for anything to happen. Da just got pissed on whiskey, the nuns pissed on sherry and, by the time he was thirteen, Derek got pissed in the garden on anything he could lay his hands on.

Clara *rises and checks her hair after the scuffle.*

Clara   This flat won't be much for him to come home to.

Jerome   I'll patch it up. It's a year since the Corporation found anyone willing to take it. Drug dealing or something gave it a bad name. It's been lying empty, with just spiders and cockroaches and bats and rats.

Clara   Ugh! After me leaving my clothes on the ground.

Jerome   There's probably an earwig snuggled down in your knickers by now.

Clara   Ugh, stop.

Jerome   I don't see why you're wriggling. He'll wind up in my moustache.

Clara   You don't have a moustache. I'm going. You're due home too.

As she turns, **Jerome** *tosses a paintbrush discreetly into one corner where it makes a loud clatter.* **Clara** *jumps back to sit beside* **Jerome** *on the bed, taking his hand. The kettle is starting to boil.*

Clara   What was that?

Jerome   I saw it move . . . (*Points.*) there . . .

Clara   Jesus, I don't want to see it.

Jerome   It's huge for its size, and there's another beside it.

Clara   Jesus, is it a rat? Say it isn't a rat.

Jerome   It isn't a rat.

Clara   A mouse?

Jerome   Not a mouse.

Clara (*still unable to look*)   What is it then?

Jerome   A bushy tailed, light brown, six-inch paintbrush.

Clara (*striking him with her fists, half laughing, half furious*)   You threw it, didn't you? You bastard.

There is another noise, freezing them both.

Clara   What's that?

Jerome   God alone knows. Whatever it is, it's more frightened of us than we should be of it. Stay, the kettle is boiled and all.

Clara (*untangling herself*)   You're like a little boy, afraid of being left alone. How long more will we really have this place?

Jerome   As often as you care to come.

Clara   I like to come regularly.

Jerome (*grabbing his shirt and starting to put it on*)   I've noticed.

Clara   But only if there's something better on offer than Earl Grey tea.

Jerome   Ginseng.

Clara   That's as strong as you go, isn't it? You're frightened of drugs, I've noticed.

Jerome (*reaching into the shopping bag for Earl Grey teabags*)   I don't need crutches.

Clara   Not 'The wild Carlow boy'. Mr Control Freak. Alex said you abandoned spirits, then wine, then red meat, white meat and cigars even. Luckily you haven't got around to women yet. How about cocaine?

Jerome (*struggling to tear open a milk carton*)   I never cared for it.

Clara   Never tried it you mean. Personally I like letting go. I go a bit wild under cocaine. If you like I'll bring some over tomorrow night.

Jerome   Tomorrow is too far away.

Clara   I wouldn't want to be late for work in the morning, would I?

Jerome   You can tell Alex I'm at a meeting till twelve, by the way.

Clara (*protests*)   But the Silverskin presentation . . . ?

Jerome   Time enough. I want to drop by here. (*Cajoling.*) Stay another ten minutes, even. Pretty please.

Clara (*teasing*)   No. Seeing as you like control so much, Jerome, it's only fair to leave the matter of how often you come before you go home tonight entirely in your own hands.

Jerome *makes a grab for her and she skips past him as lights go down to blackout.*

Scene Two

The kettle, etc, is cleared away as **Derek** *(***Jerome***'s ponytailed younger brother who is around thirty-five) enters and surveys* **Jerome** *mixing paint, with paint cans, a saw, nails, etc, now scattered around him. A hammer and an opened bag of nails rest on top of one packing case.*

Derek   Spot the fucking architect. I asked you to mind the flat not redesign it.

Jerome   Just thought I'd paint the place, Derek. How about some bright colours here for Catherine's kids and wallpaper in the far bedroom?

Derek (*indifferently, looking around for a travel bag*)   Yeah, whatever.

Jerome (*adding some white spirit*)   It needs fixing up for when you bring them back here. (*Points.*) You left your bag in the corner.

Derek (*going over to it*)   I've told you, Catherine's not planning on coming home.

Jerome (*rises*)   Then why not hand the key back to the Corporation? Stop wasting their time.

Derek *opens the travel bag and stuffs some creased shirts from one of the packing cases into it.*

Derek   What difference is it to you?

Jerome (*sitting up on a packing case to watch*)   I'm paying the bloody rent for you both.

Derek   I'll pay you back.

Jerome   I've been hearing that chorus since I was ten.

Derek   You've been throwing it back in my face since you were ten. Jerome the perfect, with an invoice book for a brain.

Jerome   I've never seen a penny nor asked for it.

Derek (*zips the bag shut angrily*)   You will. This gallery in Battersea saw slides of Catherine's installation and were hot keen. They almost even sent money for our fares.

Jerome (*reaching for his wallet.*)   Almost . . .

Derek (*insulted*)   I have the fare.

Jerome   For the boat?

Derek   The plane.

Jerome   Jesus, Derek, she doesn't have you dealing again?

Derek   Catherine could have sold a painting, you know.

Jerome   But she didn't, did she?

Derek   I earned it honestly. You're always telling me to go out and work, so why do you put me down? Why do you think I'm not capable of doing a single fucking thing for myself?

Jerome   What did you do?

Derek (*defensively*)   A job for her cousin, who has the off-licence in Rathmines. A bit of negotiating, arranging, that's all.

Jerome   Arranging what?

Derek   He has land out in Dundrum. The local residents, they're objecting to his building apartments there. The fuckers won't listen to reason or bribery. Well, Catherine says they'll listen when there's three caravan loads of knackers shitting into their back gardens from tomorrow evening.

Jerome   Are you crazy to get involved like that?

Derek   Her cousin's a decent man. He's paying the knackers four hundred quid a week. His business partner owns one of the best restaurants in town. You and Alex handled his advertising campaign when they revamped it last year. Why is it all right for you to work for him and not me?

Jerome   They're completely different things.

Derek (*picking up a spare jacket from the packing case*)   That's what Catherine said. I'm getting my hands dirty passing out envelopes on a halting site, while you sit in an office selling white lies. You were always too bloody good for the rest of us. Mammy's fucking boy living out Mammy's fucking dreams.

Jerome   Stop it.

Derek   Too stuck-up to play football on the street. Drawing away alone upstairs instead. Buildings, streets, cities. Do you ever notice how your plans never had any fucking people in them?

Jerome   At least they had straight lines, which is more than Catherine ever managed. Now that's enough.

Derek   I forgot my place, did I?

Jerome   I've refused you nothing over the years.

Derek   That's what bothers me. You could have, you know. Just because I asked, you didn't always have to make me small by giving.

Jerome   I'll not see Catherine's children starve.

Derek   This is not about them.

Jerome   Give up the amateur psychology, like you abandoned everything else, Derek. Go on, go to London.

Derek   There's opportunities over there. You needn't think we're coming back.

Jerome   I'll have the flat ready . . . just in case her genius isn't recognised again.

Derek   Are you fucking deaf or what?

There is a knock off-stage, startling them.

Derek   Who the hell is that?

Jerome   Vigilantes. Concerned Citizens Against Conceptual Art. (*Calls.*) It's open.

They watch as a **Caretaker** *in his late forties enters.*

Caretaker   Derek Furlong?

Derek   Who's looking for him?

Caretaker   I'm the caretaker in this block.

Derek   Tell the Corporation to stuff the kip, I'm away to England.

Caretaker   Who are you?

Jerome (*quickly*)   He's my brother, Jerome. He's off to a meeting in London. (*To* **Derek**, *urging him out the door.*) Go on, you'll miss your plane.

Derek *goes to tell the* **Caretaker** *the truth but stops, unsure of himself. He seems incapable of moving.*

Derek   I have the tickets, but . . . taxis, tube fares . . . I don't know if . . .

Jerome (*producing his wallet*)   Here, I owe you fifty. It will be fine. Good luck.

Derek *looks at the* **Caretaker** *one last time as if about to speak, then exits.*

Caretaker (*suspicious*)   Your brother? What's he on about?

Jerome   He's a big job, big mouth, you know. He just called in to wish us luck.

Caretaker   You'll need it. John Stiles is my brother-in-law.

Jerome   Who?

Caretaker   The official who offered you this flat. You're different from how he described you.

Jerome   He knows Catherine, my partner, mainly.

Caretaker   Aye, art school buddies. My kid sister wound up there, bringing home geezers with Dun Laoghaire accents, Auschwitz pyjamas and haircuts to cure headlice.

Jerome   We don't get to choose our in-laws.

Caretaker   A dreamer is our John. Thinking that dumping a few down-on-their-luck yuppies here will raise the tone of the place.

Jerome   Why was it empty for so long?

Caretaker   Its reputation went before it.

Jerome   Drug pushers, was it?

Caretaker   Superstition, local whispers, old wives' tales.

Jerome   I'm all right so, I don't have an old wife.

Caretaker (*looking around*)   Just a girlfriend. With two young children.

Jerome   They're shopping for beds in Bargain Town. Is there a problem?

Caretaker   Curiosity. I'm working across the corridor. John Stiles seemed surprised to see a standing order on the rent from a Guinness Mahon Bank account.

Jerome   My brother, Jerome, he's looking after me, just till my partner's career takes off. What were the local whispers about?

Caretaker   Some years back we'd a suicide here, a fourteen-year-old whose parents went off the rails. Tenants since then, they've tried using his death as an excuse to jump up the housing list. But it doesn't work. There's no try-on the Corpo hasn't heard a thousand times, from poltergeists to termites to outbreaks of plague. You don't belong here, pal. This flat should be closed off, boarded up, left alone.

Jerome   What's it to you?

Caretaker   You won't last a week here.

Jerome   I'll leave when I'm ready, 'pal', you never will.

Caretaker (*dismissively*)   I'll be around to board up when you're gone.

The **Caretaker** *exits.*

Scene Three

Soft light rises (to match the bedside lamp which comes on), as we hear the mobile phone ring. **Jerome** *sits on the bed, wearing just a pair of boxer shorts, as he answers it. He seems slightly hyper, but tries to disguise it on the phone.*

Jerome (*into the phone*)   Penny? How are you, pet? Yes, I'm in Derek's again . . . no, it's quite safe . . . I will mind myself . . . no, I'll be another few hours getting the walls finished before Catherine's kids put their grubby fingerprints all over them . . . Derek? He's grand. (**Jerome** *looks across at* **Clara** *who has emerged from the wings, in slacks and a bra*). Why don't you have a quick word with him yourself? (**Jerome** *momentarily holds the phone towards* **Clara** *who freezes, then he puts it back to his ear.*) Yes, I'll tell him. He says hello as well. I love you too. Don't wait up, you get away to bed.

He returns a kiss into the receiver, then clicks it off and looks at **Clara** *who picks up her blouse and puts it on.*

Clara   You're stoned.

Jerome (*mock Eurovision accent*)   'Effect – nul point'. (*Ordinary voice.*) Sorry. In one nostril and out the other. Earl Grey is far better.

Clara   You're holding back. I know how to let go. (*Crossly.*) You shouldn't take risks with the telephone, it's not funny.

Jerome   I never take risks. Penny hates Catherine with a passion. She never speaks to either of them.

Clara   She might feel she had to wish Derek luck in his new home. (*She looks around.*) My jacket?

Jerome (*lies back*)   Frisk me. Again. She'll send a National Gallery card, either Leech's 'Sunshade' or the fake Goosegirl one. She regards Derek as a bad influence on me as you're a good one. He'll lead me down the slope of addiction – our family failing.

Clara *spies her jacket on the floor, picks it up then kneels beside him on the bed.*

Clara   Show me your eyes.

Jerome   Mrs Beecham's Powders would have more effect.

Clara   You should be stoned . . . or more stoned at least . . .

Jerome   It shows I'm not cut out for the supermarket business. Two snorts of cocaine and I've no desire to share my bath with Orlando Trailer Park white trash. (*He grabs her.*) Or throw myself from the balcony, taking my mistress with me.

She struggles to break free, then laughs.

Clara   Bastard. I'm not your mistress.

Jerome   Then what are you?

Clara (*stepping away and taking cigarettes from her bag*)   I'm myself. The woman you're currently screwing.

Jerome   For how long?

Clara (*lights up and blows smoke at him*)   As long as you still interest me and don't keel over from throat cancer. Just because I've screwed you doesn't mean I've cracked you yet. Mistresses went out with the Middle Ages, which means you're just about old enough to remember them.

Jerome   I remember everything, even going to a dance in Thomastown with my father and going home with my mother.

Clara   Very careless.

Jerome   Very Irish. Even with nuns in the family.

Clara   You and Penny . . . ?

Jerome   What?

Clara   I would have thought that kids might have suited you.

Jerome   You would have thought wrong. Not everybody needs appendages. Penny and I are happy.

Clara   You're very different, the pair of you.

Jerome   We're suited. I always thought I'd marry a Yank or one of those English girls with long legs and hyphens in their surnames. I settled for a rich Protestant instead. In-built class, poise, compassion for the poor.

Clara   Penny's family are nice.

Jerome   Her grandfather says to me once on his crumbling verandah, (*Mock voice.*) 'Of course Balbriggan's population has declined these last years.' (*Own voice.*) All I can see across the fields are new Council estates everywhere. I think he's going senile, then I realise he means there's a dozen less horse Prods tottering around the place. (*Mock voice.*) 'Malahide has quite a big population still, but they're not really our sort.' (*Own voice.*) This time he's not even discussing Catholics. Whatever class of Protestant lives in Malahide isn't good enough for him. The walking fucking dead, eh?

Clara   I'll give you 'Walking Dead'.

Laughing, she makes as if to plant a love bite on his neck. He stills her suddenly, alert and animated.

Jerome   Stop.

Clara   I'm not stupid enough to leave a mark.

Jerome   No. I mean that's it. The perfect pitch.

Clara   What?

Jerome   For the meeting with Silverskin in the morning.

Clara   You've lost me.

Jerome   Alex's storyline is staid. A twenty-second pan down some naked girl's back to a tight bikini shot plays like an ad for condoms, hints of sex, then dire warnings. It's a campaign for men around a product mainly bought by women. We're taking the client for granted.

Clara   What are you suggesting?

Throwing himself around the bed, **Jerome** *acts out his idea.*

Jerome   A thirty-second silent movie starts with gothic organ chords, lightning flashing through a castle window. A door creaks open to reveal a coffin covered with flecks of clay. (*He holds up the blanket and slowly covers his face with it.*) The lid begins to close over.

Clara *laughs and climbs on to the bed as well, horse playing, not taking him seriously.*

Clara   No earthly connection to the product. Silverskin will love this.

Jerome   Faithful servants enter who lift the coffin in silence. (*Hops around the bed.*) Flash forward to a ship's hold. Rats scurry as dawn breaks. We hear a distant scream (*His face and hand appear, managing to snatch the cigarette from her hand, over her silent protests.*) as a black cloak flashes past and the coffin lid closes over. (*He covers himself with the blanket again.*) Flash forward again – the exterior of a villa beside a crowded beach. Then, a snap interior, in the cellar the faithful servants have the coffin open, they work away, massaging the body inside with a lotion we cannot see. They step back. (*He drops the blanket and rises dramatically, holding the fragments of her stubbed out cigarette as fangs.*) Dracula slowly rises, smiling through his fangs, dressed in his bathing suit and clutching a bottle of Silverskin Factor Thirty sun cream. Exterior closing shot, Dracula, cavorting on the beach, surrounded by bikinied babes. Then the caption, in Century Gothic type – 'Silverskin, Factor Thirty, the ultimate protection.'

Clara *collapses in laughter, then looks up, realising he is totally serious.*

Clara   That's absolutely brilliant. Why didn't you think of it with Alex?

Jerome   Alex never gives me love bites. You write it up tonight, storyboard it, show it to him in the morning.

Clara   What do you mean?

Jerome   You like it, you have it. Tell Alex it's yours. You want to get ahead, Clara, take any chances that are given you.

Clara   But it's your idea.

Jerome   Three months ago you started as a receptionist. I've told Alex you've hidden talents, but I can't promote you without his approval. When Stephen Roche rode his first Tour de France he was wrecked peddling up some mountain. This fat little man ran alongside him, pushing the bike, and whispering 'I do this because I know you'll never need anyone's help again.' Think of me as that small fat man.

Clara   What if Alex doesn't like it?

Jerome   I'll be there at nine a.m. to back you up.

Clara   Don't be late. The presentation is at ten.

Jerome   It's early still. (*He lies back on the bed.*) Don't go yet.

Clara (*peering out the window*)   For God's sake, Jerome, I've only a few hours to do the presentation up. I can see my taxi pulling in, the driver won't wait around.

Jerome   Call one later. Just another ten minutes. You said cocaine makes it better for you.

Clara (*laughs*)   I know your ten minutes. The world is on the tear tonight before Good Friday. I'm taking no chances of taxis not coming here after midnight.

Jerome   Judas.

Clara   You're a star for the idea. Thanks.

She blows him a kiss and exits. **Jerome** *lies back in the bed and* *pulls the quilt over him. Now that she is gone, he admits to himself that the drugs have had an effect and snorts loudly, trying to clear his head.*

Jerome   Wooosh . . . cocaine isn't bad stuff actually. I must be mad, giving ideas away. Clear the head. Ten minutes rest, then home.

He clicks off the bedside light, leaving the stage in almost total darkness, except for a shaft of light as if through a window. After a moment, there's a creak, before one of two unopened tins of paint (on their sides near the wall) trundles noisily across the raked floor.

He switches on the bedside lamp and looks at the paint tin, perturbed. He gets out of bed and puts it back, upright, against the wall. He turns the other can upright as well, then glances at the floor, wondering if there is a slant. The bedside lamp flickers off by itself. **Jerome** *rises, slightly unnerved, and picks the lamp up. It flickers back on.*

Jerome   (*to himself, putting it back down*)   Loose connection. (*Shakes his head.*) Fuck it, I hate drugs. A taxi out of here.

He pulls a sweatshirt on and reaches for his mobile phone. He dials, listens and dials again, then stares at the phone.

Jerome   (*annoyed*)   I only charged the batteries yesterday. (*He glances towards where the window would be.*) What chance of a rank around here?

The precariously balanced top case in the pile of packing cases in one corner topples over suddenly, with a loud bang, startling **Jerome**, *who drops the phone and turns.*

Jerome   (*calls*)   Who's there? Who's after getting in here? (*He looks around.*) Clara? (*To himself.*) Fuck it, she left the door open. (*He reaches into a packing case and produces a baseball bat which he slaps against his palm.*) Come on, local reception committee, let's see what you're made of. One of yous, two of yous. Come on, chicken-shit. (*He circles cagily till he relaxes, convinced he is alone.*) Rats. The place must be infested with them. (*Mock BBC accent.*) 'One Man and his Rodent – a gripping new series for BBC Two with sheep-pens designed by the noted retired architect, Jerome Furlong.'

He picks up his mobile phone and tries it again. He tosses the phone in disgust back towards the bed and moves across the room as if to glance out the window.

Jerome *(peering down)*   Fuck it, there is a cider appreciation committee meeting down on the steps. Easy knowing Thursday is dole day. Think I'll pass up the chance to broaden my palate and wait till these gougers have moved on.

He gets back into bed, pulling the quilt over him and switches out the bedside lamp. As the stage plunges into moonlight, a gauze behind the bed is lit so that the faint silhouette of a young boy's body is revealed, hanging by the neck from a rope. **Jerome** *drifts towards sleep, unaware of it. A hammer and bag of nails are plainly visible on top of a packing case in the direct ray of moonlight. The plastic bag of nails suddenly turns over, spilling on to the floor.* **Jerome** *sleeps on, oblivious to it. Then the hammer falls and we hear it slide across the floorboards. The silhouette fades, as there is five seconds of utter silence, broken by a piercing shriek of agony from* **Jerome**.

With great difficulty he manages to switch on the bedside lamp, using the thumb of his left hand. In the light we see the quilt is stained with blood and glistening six-inch nails pierce the palms of both his left hand (beside the lamp) and his right hand (lying upright at the far extremity of the bed). He stares at them and screams again in agony as the stage plunges into blackout.

Scene Four

A row of three chairs at the left front of stage to suggest a hospital casualty department. **Jerome** *enters, stage left, and sits on the end chair in the row, sunk into himself, his hands bound in bloodstained bandages.*

Penny *(an attractive woman in her mid to late thirties) enters from top stage right, deeply worried, while a white-coated* **Doctor** *enters top stage left. They speak as they walk, until gradually their two paths merge, with their opening lines allowing the audience time and speculation to adjust to moving beyond the confines of the flat into a black box setting. As the scene develops we sense an inner strength within* **Penny**.

Doctor   Any history of epilepsy?

Penny   No.

Doctor   Coronary thrombosis? Palpitations? Low blood pressure?

Penny   No. What has happened?

Doctor   Chronic fatigue? Paranoia? Schizophrenia?

Penny   What has happened to my husband?

Doctor   Has he bad debts? Business problems?

Penny (*reaching him and placing a hand on his arm*)   Doctor, I asked you a question.

Doctor   I wish I could answer it, Mrs Furlong. (*He stops and points towards* **Jerome**.) He appears to have walked from Ballymun into the Mater Hospital earlier tonight. The doctors there say they removed two six-inch nails from his palms and gave him a tetanus injection after stitching the wounds up. They couldn't even get him to fill out an admissions form before he vanished. He arrived here at Beaumont half an hour ago, losing blood like someone had split the wounds back open. Your address was in his wallet. It's crammed with credit cards, so robbery isn't a motive. Strictly speaking I should phone the police, but Shane . . . one of the junior doctors . . . recognised him from Doheny and Nesbitt's pub. Let's just say your husband isn't the usual type we get wandering in from Ballymun. I wouldn't want to cause any difficulties with the police . . . unless it was necessary.

Penny   Let me talk to him.

Doctor   He's in shock.

The **Doctor** *steps back and exits as* **Penny** *tentatively approaches* **Jerome** *who looks up, but hardly seems to take her in.*

Penny   Jerome . . . are you okay? (*She leans down.*) Darling, it's me.

Jerome (*quietly*)   Penny.

Penny *takes his bandaged hand tenderly in her own.*

Penny (*shocked and concerned*)   Who did this to you? Your poor hands. Your fingers . . . thank God they're not broken. Who hurt you? (*No reply.*) Why are you too scared to answer? Jerome, look at me . . . please.

Jerome   Back here . . . in this bloody hospital again . . .

Penny   You're okay now, I've come to bring you home. Just talk to me . . . please. (*Sudden anger.*) It's Derek's fault, isn't it? What trouble is he after getting you into now? Where is he? Derek's in debt again, isn't he? Then why isn't he here with you? Why isn't he the one hurt?

Jerome (*dazed, withdrawn, in shock*)   Not Derek.

Penny   Who then? (*No reply.*) Why are you so afraid? I never saw you afraid of anything. How many did it take to hold you down like that? The cowardly bastards!

Jerome   No one.

Penny   What are you saying? (*No reply.*) Jerome, do you want me to phone the police?

Jerome   They can't help me.

Penny   I'll call Clara. It's almost dawn, but she won't mind.

Jerome   No, please.

Penny   Clara's your friend, mine too. We can trust her. I need to talk to somebody. I'm scared. Why did these men hurt you?

Jerome   The flat . . .

Penny   Derek's flat?

Jerome   I didn't know such things were real before . . . the hair on my neck stiffening.

Penny (*scared*)   Is Derek still in the flat? Did they leave him for dead?

Jerome (*distressed*)   Sweet God Almighty.

Penny (*panicking*)   Catherine's children, are they hurt?

Jerome   Gone, all gone away. My hands hurt.

Penny (*looks*)   They're starting to bleed again. That doctor swore they'd stemmed the blood properly this time. Where are Derek and the children?

Jerome   England. Left this morning. Please God it was the cocaine.

Penny (*trying to follow him*)   Is Derek dealing in cocaine?

Jerome   I've got to make sense of it. (*He looks at her.*) I'm going mad, Penny, I've lost my reason.

Penny   Just tell me who did this to you.

Jerome   I did . . . I must have . . . by myself . . . without even feeling the first nail. Hammers and nails can't move by themselves . . . Trailer Park white trash . . .

Penny   What Trailer Park? Was some woman involved?

Jerome (*fiercely*)   I refuse to go mad. I'll stay in control, I shall be sane.

Penny (*terrified*)   I'm phoning Clara. Darling, I need someone here with me.

Jerome (*distressed, lifting his hands*)   Just make these wounds stop bleeding.

Distressed, **Penny** *rises and looks round for the vanished doctor.*

Penny   I'll call a nurse . . . don't move . . .

She exits stage left, seeking help. **Jerome** *is left alone staring at his bandaged hands in terror, as* **Rita** *(a woman in her fifties) enters and sits on the third seat, slumped in exhaustion for a moment. She looks across at* **Jerome**.

Rita   Mister, you're bleeding. (*No response.*) I said, you're bleeding.

Jerome   What's it to you?

Rita   You're making a mess. Some woman has to wash the floor after you.

Jerome   Just leave me alone.

Rita (*hurt*)   Bleed to death so. You just might have the decency to do it on your own floor.

They sit apart for a moment before **Rita** *reaches into her bag for cigarettes. She looks around guiltily, then lights up. She looks across at* **Jerome** *and offers him one.*

Rita   Here, mister. (**Jerome** *shakes his head.*) No, you're all right. That's why I come down here from the children's ward. This time of night there's never any nurses around to tell you to put it out.

Jerome *looks at her again, then takes one and accepts a light from her. He inhales deeply.*

Rita   That's better, isn't it? Are you waiting for someone else? (*He shakes his head.*) I'm just waiting, hanging about. God knows, I know every corridor of this place.

Jerome   The yard at the back . . . that's the best place to smoke. (*She looks at him surprised.*) You can sit alone there for hours at night, no one to bother you.

Rita   That's right.

Jerome   Total quiet. Just twenty-eight steps.

Rita   What is?

Jerome   From the first floor corridor to the back yard. Fourteen, then a bend on the stairs, then fourteen more. The worst coffee in the world in that machine on the bend.

Rita   Who are you telling, Mister? What happened to your hands?

Jerome   A cable slipped, I cut them.

Rita   Will I call a nurse? You need them seen to.

Jerome   No. Enjoy your smoke in peace.

Rita (*bitter half laugh*)   What would I know about peace, Mister? (*Looks at him.*) Sorry, I shouldn't be bothering strangers. It's the nerves, I can't stop talking. If I had the courage to smoke in there, I'd stick to that poky wee chapel across the way.

Jerome (*looks back to where* **Penny** *has exited*)   I have to go.

Rita (*putting out a hand to restrain him*)   You can't go anywhere like that, for God's sake. (*Glances behind as well.*) Was it a fight you were in or what?

Jerome   A cable, I told you.

Rita   Here. (*She holds the packet out.*) Have a couple of ciggies if you want, it looks like you'll be here till dawn. (*He shakes his head and she withdraws the packet.*) I'm away home to Ballymun. I've been here all night so my daughter could get some sleep. She's back in, but I can see by her she didn't sleep a wink.

Jerome   Who's ill?

Rita   My granddaughter, Jacinta, she has cystic fibrosis. We've never known how long we'll have her for, how long her lungs will last. She's been on a waiting list for months for a transplant. She's critical up in the ward now, I can't see her last beyond another day or two. It's a terrible thing to pray for, that some other family be devastated by tragedy, some child be knocked down, that from somewhere, if it's God's will, a donor organ will be found. Is it any wonder that half the time I can't even pray?

Jerome   Don't bother. You might as well be talking to the speaking clock, except at least the speaking clock answers back.

Rita (*caustically*)   Is that right? So what do you believe in, Smarty-pants?

Jerome   My own eyes . . . logic . . . reason. That objects can't move by themselves, wounds don't keep re-opening.

Rita   You're half cracked, you know that.

Jerome (*looks at her*)   Say it again.

Rita (*worried*)   Ah now, Mister.

Jerome   I won't be offended, I just wish to God it was true. (*He shows her his bandaged hand.*) This happened to me in Ballymun.

Rita   With a cable?

Jerome   No cable. I woke up in McBride Tower around midnight to see a boy in a blue jacket leaning over me, just for the flick of an eyelid. 'Play Jesus for me,' he said. 'Play Jesus.' Then the bastard was gone and there was a burst of pain as nails were hammered into my flesh.

Rita   Good Christ! Not the flat on the twelfth floor?

Jerome   How did you know?

Rita (*scared*)   Who doesn't know? I thought it was boarded up still. You should see a priest.

Jerome   I don't like priests, I don't believe. (*He leans towards her, holding his hands out, undoing the bandages.*) Look. Tell me again that I'm stark raving mad. Say it's lunacy to believe that these could somehow be the wounds of Christ!

Rita (*backing away with a sharp intake of breath*)   I don't know, Mister. How the hell would I know? I just came in here for a quiet smoke.

Jerome   Twice tonight I've walked half way to Malahide before the pain got too much. When I unpeel these bandages there's a clot of blood on each palm, congealed into the shape of a nailhead. And fresh blood oozing from beneath the stitches again.

Rita (*frightened*)   What are you saying, Mister?

Jerome   That I can't believe my own eyes. Mobile phones are miracles, cloned sheep are miracles, Viagra is a miracle for those who need a bloody miracle. Logical miracles. But not this . . . not some . . . (*He looks at her, coming to his senses and withdrawing his hands.*) I'm sorry. I didn't mean to frighten you. It's just that all night I've been too afraid to talk to anyone.

Rita   I'm only a cleaner. Sure I can't help you.

Jerome   I know.

Rita   And Matt Talbot was only a labourer. My mother remembered him collapsing down Gramby Lane, with rumours of rusty chains in his flesh. Our teacher in Brunswick Street used to say he'd seen Matt urinating and begging on the streets. 'If they can call that drunkard a saint,' he'd say, 'any of yous can become one.'

Jerome   What use is a saint?

Rita   What use is a doctor either?

Jerome   What do you mean?

Rita   When you're in trouble you need to talk to somebody. Those foreign saints, I wouldn't know what to be saying to them. But Matt was one of our own. He wouldn't ignore an old neighbour. You mock all you like, Mister, but I pray to Matt because he knows suffering, he suffered for us all. Well, I've suffered enough and there's more chance of Matt Talbot helping my Jacinta than the doctors here being able to do anything for her. (*She looks at* **Jerome**.) I've to go, Mister, I've offices to clean soon, but Jacinta Boyle is her name. Will you pray for her too?

Jerome   I've told you, I don't pray.

Rita *hesitates, then reaches over to touch the fresh blood on* **Jerome**'s *hand. She touches her finger against her forehead, leaving a red speck there.*

Rita   Being stubborn doesn't make you any more of a man, Mister. So maybe just this one time you will. That flat is dangerous, stay away from it.

Jerome   'Play Jesus for me,' he said. 'Play Jesus.' (*Looks back again towards where* **Penny** *has vanished.*) I have to go.

He shakes his head and exits. **Rita** *looks behind her as* **Penny** *re-enters, top left, with the* **Doctor**. **Rita** *hurriedly stubs out her cigarette and exits.* **Penny** *and the* **Doctor** *stare at the empty chairs. Blackout.*

Scene Five

The ringing of a mobile phone breaks the blackout. **Jerome** *sits on a park bench, stage right, staring at his bandaged hands. He takes the phone from his pocket, stares at it, goes to answer but finds he hasn't the courage. It stops ringing and he puts it back. A* **Down-and-out** *crosses the stage, face half-hidden by a monkey hat, holding a can of beer and pulling at the very butt-end of a cigarette which is almost burning his fingertips. He reluctantly stubs it out, sitting down on the bench as the phone starts to ring again. He breaks into a smoker's cough and spits as* **Jerome** *moves up to get away from him. The* **Down-and-out** *notices and moves up too, staring at* **Jerome** *as the phone keeps ringing.*

Down-and-out   Are you bleeding deaf, pal?

Jerome   What?

Down-and-out (*points at the phone*)   I think it's for you. I told the Missus never to phone me at work.

Jerome   It will stop ringing soon. It always does.

Down-and-out   You got a smoke, no?

Jerome   No.

Down-and-out   'Ere the price of a few cans?

Jerome   I'm afraid not.

Down-and-out   You're about as much use as a nun's tit.

Jerome *looks at the ringing mobile phone a last time, then rises and tosses it across to the* **Down-and-out**.

Jerome (*going to exit*)   Here, I've a mobile phone.

Down-and-out (*Instinctively catching it*)   Shag off with that yoke, they give you bleeding cancer.

Stunned by the gift of the phone, the **Down-and-out** *stares after the departing* **Jerome**.

Down-and-out   Hey, next time you make a bridge at snooker try running the cue between your fingers, not bleeding through them. (*He picks up the phone.*) Hello? (*Mock voice.*) Who's speaking please? Grafton, Giles and who? Well, fuck off, Grafton, Giles and Who. Hang on, you haven't got a newspaper there? Call us out a few numbers for those bleeding sex lines at the back.

Lights go down as he is talking, so his speech fades away into semi-blackout. **Down-and-out** *exits.*

Scene Six

Jerome *re-enters the flat cautiously, as if summoning courage. There is a bottle in a paper bag in his pocket and he seems slightly drunk. He surveys the room in silence, then looks across, startled by a noise in the wings, to see* **Clara** *emerge.*

Clara   You've surfaced at last. Penny phoned from the hospital. I persuaded her against calling the police but I don't know for how much longer. Where have you been?

Jerome   I haven't walked so far since I was a child. The things you see when you're going nowhere. People in Casualty, how they queue like sheep; a man crying openly on the hospital steps; junkies in the entrance, shivering, waiting for their methadone. How the glass doors slide open by themselves – me and this girl of four spent half an hour just sitting, watching them.

Clara   What were you doing?

Jerome   I took a day off from my life. Is that so terrible?

Clara   Yes. When I didn't know what was happening this morning, trying to sell Alex that pitch for Silverskin alone, it is. When I had to take your place beside him at the meeting with them it is. When Penny is in bits it is. I've been with her half the day, calling your mobile, waiting by the phone.

Jerome   How long are you here?

Clara   Since midnight.

Jerome (*looks around*)   Have you felt anything here, seen anyone?

Clara   I should never have given you cocaine. I blame myself.

Jerome   This has nothing to do with you.

Clara   You weren't used to drugs.

Jerome   What did Penny tell you?

Clara   That somebody attacked your hands. She thinks you're in trouble. (*Beat.*) Are you?

Jerome   Trouble deep.

Clara   How much do you owe?

Jerome   Nothing.

Clara   Who attacked you then? Did you go walkabout around these towers after I left? You know how dangerous . . .

Jerome   It happened in here. In my sleep I hammered six-inch nails through my palms.

Clara   Save the lies for your wife, Jerome. This is me you're talking to.

Jerome   Then you explain it, Clara. You were the last person here. Nobody did this to me. I'm running from nobody, I'm scared of nobody. (*Beat.*) Except I'm so scared shitless it took three hours to find the courage in a bottle to come up here.

Clara   The cocaine screwed you up. Have you eaten?

Jerome   I'm fasting.

Clara *laughs, then realises he is serious.*

Clara   For what?

Jerome   My soul. Or his. Whoever's soul you fast for when you're playing Jesus.

Clara   Were you and Alex laundering money, is that it?

Jerome   I simply write jingles for ads.

Clara   We don't call them jingles.

Jerome   They sound like jingles, they go round and round in my head. Unreal tunes for unreal lives. I need you to believe me. Something entered my bloodstream last night. It's there still, pumping round my heart.

Clara   Cocaine.

Jerome   God.

Clara   What?

Jerome   Or the devil or some manifestation I don't understand but which shouldn't be here. God should be like the measles, a short childhood illness we can't get twice. He went out with black and white TV. But can't you feel it around you? Something good or diabolical or both. Something in this flat, watching us.

Clara   Jerome, listen to me . . .

Jerome   You listen. I've spent all day hiding, trying to put sufficient distance between myself and this place but my feet kept turning back.

Clara (*trying to calm him*)   You're having a nervous breakdown. It's nothing to be ashamed of. We can get help.

Jerome   Could I really just be going crazy? Wouldn't that be wonderful?

Clara   You work hard, and even if you and Alex don't realise it, business isn't booming. If you're not moving forwards you're going backwards fast. The pressure got to you, maybe other pressures too. Come home. Penny is waiting.

Jerome   I can't face her. I saw the light up here. I knew it had to be you, but I sat on a wall drinking. I was afraid of ghosts if you weren't here, afraid of ridicule if you were.

Clara   You're simply not well. There's nothing here.

Jerome (*shivers*)   Is that all you feel? Nothing? His pain is all around you, like a wall of ice.

Clara   Whose pain?

Jerome   The boy who attacked me. The boy in the blue jacket.

Clara   You're rambling, Jerome.

Jerome   He's still here, trapped. He can't find his way to Christ.

Clara   That's enough. (*She holds out the phone.*) We need to phone Penny. You know you never wanted to hurt her.

Jerome   How can I answer her questions when the answers make no sense? (*He looks around, almost in a world of his own.*) Can you not feel how cold the room has become?

Clara (*slightly unnerved*)   Come away. I want to mind you.

Jerome (*coldly, trying to gain back control*)   I don't need minding. If you feel nothing, then just go.

Clara   You can't stay. Look at your hands.

Jerome   All day I've tried convincing myself I'm crazy, but I see things with a clarity I haven't known since childhood. (*Looks at her.*) Have a drink with me.

Clara   No.

Jerome   Go on, have a fag as well. There's a glass in that packing case.

Reluctantly **Clara** *goes across and gets one as* **Jerome** *sits down.*

Jerome (*almost to himself*)   How did I ever come to be sitting here?

Clara *holds her glass out and he pours her a whiskey. She sits apart from him as he takes a slug himself from the bottle.*

Jerome (*a jingly sing-song voice*)

> Buy a car from us,
> They're really rather cheap,
> Chance your luck with a Glenageary slut
> In the back of our two-ton jeep.

Clara   Stop mocking yourself.

Jerome   Everything I've done for years is a mockery. I used to be somebody in Carlow, even if Da drank. I stood out from the bogmen with their shiny suits crusted in dandruff. I had a destiny. Let other mothers want a priest in their family. Let them all have bishops for their daddies for all my mother cared, with two nuns already in the bank. Nobody else would have an architect. I remember how I'd finish studying and stand in the garden, looking down at the lights of the town. I was twelve and I knew I was going to be someone.

He drinks again, deeply.

When did I stop knowing? Da playing the organ in the cathedral, dropping notes, wheezing, sobered up and shaved by my mother. I was so ashamed of him, yet always trying to make him proud. (*He looks at Clara.*) I'm rambling, amn't I?

Clara   You're not well, Jerome.

Jerome   It's what he did, mumbling away to himself in the hospice when he was dying. Scraps of prayers that made me embarrassed. Could he not accept what's coming for us all, once the nurses kept the pain at bay? Drifting in and out of consciousness. He woke one time, fingers beckoning. I thought he was going to ask me to kneel down. I would have too, if he'd wanted. I wasn't some stuck-up Dublin would-be tenor with a neck like a jockey's bollix. (*Dying father's voice.*) 'So proud of you, son, all you're going to do.' (*Own voice.*) I'd have given my right hand to spare him one second of that pain. Don't ask me why but I loved that sad shambles of a man who'd spent his life trying to smell of Fox's Glacier Mints.

Clara   My mother died. I know what it feels like.

Jerome (*looks at her*)   You know nothing about me, nothing.

Clara   I know it's logical to feel guilt, even years afterwards.

Jerome   What has logic to do with anything? Explain this with your logic. (*Undoing the bandage on one hand.*) Tell me I'm sufficiently neurotic to inflict this on myself. (**Clara** *looks at his palm and backs away slightly.*) Touch it.

Clara (*scared*)   No.

Jerome   The wound has opened wide enough to place your finger into it.

Clara (*disgusted*)   It's a running sore. It's disgusting.

Jerome   We've fucked in hotel beds, in Penny's bed that weekend she was away, across my office desk when Alex's back was turned. You took my cock in your mouth, you swallowed my come. Can't you even bring yourself to place one finger on this wound?

Clara   The sight of blood makes me sick. I don't know what's happening, but I know doctors. You need help, Jerome.

Jerome   I need you to believe what's in front of your eyes.

Clara   Maybe you couldn't take the secrecy of our affair. Maybe that's why you mutilated yourself and are afraid to go home. But you never had to choose. I'd never have asked you to leave Penny.

Jerome   I could have my cake and eat it, is that it? What if God plays by different rules?

Clara   There's no God, only guilt. There are delusions and drugs to cure them.

Jerome   Tell Penny I'm okay, I just need time to sort things out.

Clara (*holding out her mobile phone*)   Tell her yourself.

Jerome (*beat*)   I'm too ashamed.

Clara (*lowering the phone*)   What about Alex?

Jerome   Screw Alex, if you haven't done so already.

Clara (*deeply hurt*)   Bastard.

Jerome (*apologetically*)   I'm sorry. That was uncalled for.

Clara   Funny how God and hypocrisy always go hand in hand.

Jerome   I'm being honest. I should have letters after my name for hypocrisy these last years, a Master's degree. But even I can't fathom you. All this trying to get close to Penny, bringing desserts over for our dinner parties, I never understood it. I mean we were just about sex, weren't we?

Clara   If I was screwing my way to the top why bother with you? For years you've been stuck in an elevator between floors afraid to move.

Jerome   Why did you bother?

Clara   Maybe I liked screwing in elevators. Maybe there was more going on if you hadn't shut everything else.

Jerome   I was open with you.

Clara   You were a closed shop, even to yourself. Do you ever look at your knuckles? They're white from gripping on to everything. That's not stigmata, it's neurosis you can't face up to. (*Looks around.*) There are no devils or angels here, only consumers at the lowest end of the market, those hardly worth pitching ads at except for sliced bread and Yellow Pack cornflakes. You couldn't handle cocaine and maybe you couldn't handle me, the fact that I wanted nothing from you. No commitment, no favours. But you've always needed to be needed. Look at you here, painting a flat for kids that aren't even your own. You used to make me laugh, like a boy trying to be grown-up. But you couldn't handle freedom. You've gone daft, Jerome, a breakdown cloaked in self-delusions of grandeur.

Jerome   You should just go.

Clara   Come with me. Even if some ghost is here then what's it to do with you?

Jerome   I don't know. But I'm not leaving here until I see this through.

Clara   You're pissed. I'll tell Penny it's the old family failing. Sleep it off, Jerome, then go home.

Clara *retreats off stage as lights go down.*

Scene Seven

A solitary light comes up on **Jerome** *sitting on a packing case beside the bed. The bedside lamp is on. It is not long before dawn. The bottle of whiskey from his pocket is now almost finished. It rests at his feet, although he takes a slug occasionally.* **Jerome** *looks around, addressing the empty space.*

Jerome (*quietly and drunkenly*)   All right, pal, it's just you and me now. I'll say it one last time, (*Calls.*) 'Coo-ee, anyone home?' (*He looks around.*) Come on, boy, don't be shy, I've seen you already. You wanted me to play Jesus for you. So here I am, you little prick.

He takes a slug, his voice both confiding and menacing.

Don't fuck with me. Come out! The other tenants may have been scared chicken-shit, but you took no chances, eh? You nailed me to the floor. The ultimate captive audience. I've found out things about you, I asked in that barn of a pub at closing time. You're quite a local celebrity. In Kerry they'd build a festival around you. But here even the junkies wouldn't come into this flat to shoot up. They say you hanged yourself. (*He drinks.*) That takes courage, but maybe you didn't mean to jump, maybe you were acting out a fantasy and slipped? I've known the odd fall myself. (*He takes a long slug.*) I don't think it was courage. I think you just reacted when your father died, more frightened of being left alone than of a broken neck.

He drinks again, getting into his stride.

I've always run away from pain personally. I don't mind

dying, it's indignity that frightens me, shitting into bedpans, primeval visitors arriving from Carlow with grapes. Can't say I fancy burial either, you wouldn't know where the worms have been. No, a discreet cremation followed by oblivion. I'm fastidious, not a peeping Tom like you.

Maybe spying on Clara and me got you jealous? You probably always wondered what sex was like? I hate to say it, kid, but it's better than you ever imagined. I know because I've had it and you never will because you're dead, and poltergeists don't frighten me. (*He rises challengingly.*) You see, I'm not scared of the dead, I'm not running from anything. Come on, show yourself! (*He circles cagily.*) What's the problem, you never confronted a real man before? Only cowards hang themselves. Chicken Licken.

Jerome *picks up the bottle again and looks at it.*

Look what you've reduced me to, my daddy's son. In the pub they looked at me differently like I'd been in a fight. People I wouldn't notice before. People like you. The white sock brigade at job placement interviews. Rule number one, weed out the blebs wearing cheap white socks first.

The bedside lamp suddenly switches off by itself. **Jerome** *turns, startled, trying to rein in his fear.*

Did I strike a nerve? Bit of a snob at heart, were you? Must have been hard with your daddy a lush. (*The lamp flickers again.*) What's wrong, you expected sympathy? You're dead and there's fuck all I can do about it. I bet you never had the guts to knock over his drink, eh? That would not have been wise. I know, you see, all about hiding bottles in wardrobes or fearing he'd discover the money hidden for food or he'd raise his voice so the neighbours would hear. Mummy didn't want us to lose our place amongst the Carlow intelligentsia – a singularly select and self-appointed bunch with bad gums – not that Derek ever cared. I know all about shame and whispers down the tennis club where you needed two cars in the driveway to have any chance of a hand-job behind the nets after a dance.

He looks at the lamp.

Go on, flicker the lamp. Don't pretend that didn't get your attention. Hand-jobs weren't all they were cracked up to be. Big agricultural wrists with too much topspin. Actually nothing was what it was cracked up to be. I know Clara boasts about the smart clients she can attract in Temple Bar, but Dublin is still just a provincial terminus on the Carlow train line. Don't get me wrong though. You'd have settled for half what I have and lived happily. So let's stop these stupid manifestations, eh? Amateur theatrics don't scare me. Even this sudden coldness, like a deep-freeze.

He takes a slug of whiskey and looks around.

Your existence has me rattled though, boy. You're cheating me of oblivion. But the bottom line is that you picked the wrong guy to play Jesus. There's probably some hocus-pocus ritual to send you on your travels, but I just do advertising jingles. So make these ridiculous wounds stop bleeding, then you and I can go back to our own limbos.

He reaches over to touch the lamp, which flickers. He shakes it again and it flickers once more. He turns if off in disgust.

A loose connection that Derek was too lazy to fix. You're not even here, kid, are you? I'm talking to myself. (*He sits down and takes a slug.*) Clara's right, I'm having a breakdown, hammering nails in my own hands. Is this how much I hate myself? (*He looks around.*) I should phone Penny, I'm going crazy like Da mumbling in the dark. (*Dying father's voice.*) 'You'll call the baby after me, son, won't you?' (*Own voice.*) 'He'll be the spit of you too, Da, I bet. You'll never be dead when my child comes into the world.'

He looks at his bloodied palms.

Nine months of waiting, my hand on her stomach, feeling the bump, the faintest kicks. Then those eight God-awful days, those God-awful days. (*Looks up.*) Don't talk to me about grief, whatever you are. (*Takes a slug.*) Penny would conceive again, she kept saying, when she could finally speak. We'd be a family again. The awful hope in her voice hurt more than anything. The only thing that came back was my seed undelivered, marked 'recipient gone away, no forwarding address given'. There was just a monotonous ache that went on until I stopped noticing it. Not even screwing Clara was an escape, only part of the same routine, life by numbers. 'Fiddle the books, fiddle the taxman, fiddle the wife. Fiddle yourself into believing you're still alive.'

He looks around.

Are you listening to me, empty silence, electrical manufacturers' fault? It wasn't some ghost I saw here when I was stoned. It was the stupid kid that I once was, come back to haunt me. Guilt and cocaine did the rest. It's time for home with my tail between my legs. Doctors, rest and another squalid secret to cover up.

He smiles bitterly and takes another slug. Suddenly the bottle is tugged from his mouth and smashes against the wall. The packing case he sits on tumbles over, throwing him on to his knees, while other objects get thrown about in one continuous motion. **Jerome** *looks around in terror, then raises his freely bleeding hand as if protecting his eyes against a brilliant glare.*

Jerome *(terrified)*   Who's out there? Who's doing this to me? I never gave consent, you understand? I do not believe in you . . . I refuse . . . refuse . . . do you hear? You cannot just barge in on my life . . . fuck you, blast you, whoever you are. I will not serve . . . *(Beat, terror gives way to bafflement.)* If you want his soul so much then come in for him your bloody self, because how the hell do I know how to bring him to you. It's not my problem, so why have you chosen me, Christ? Why does it have to be me?

Act Two

Scene One

When lights come up the stage may be bare if the 'flat' set is portable. Otherwise the 'flat' is simply unlit. **Penny** *appears front stage right as* **Jerome** *enters front stage left and approaches her.*

Penny (*angry and relieved*)   Where have you been all yesterday and last night? Me like a fool, making excuses on the phone, worrying myself sick. Were the hell where you?

Jerome   I should have phoned. I'm sorry.

Penny   Clara stopped me contacting the police. She said you weren't in danger, you just had things to sort out. I didn't know what to believe. She wouldn't say who drove those nails through your hands.

Jerome   If I tell you the truth you won't respect me anymore. I don't care what else I lose but I never wanted to lose your respect, even if I don't deserve it.

Penny   I'm your wife. If you can't trust me who can you trust?

Jerome *slowly holds his hands out towards her.*

Jerome   A poltergeist made these holes, the ghost of a boy. They ache constantly, yet it's only a fraction of the pain his spirit is in.

Penny (*long beat, quietly, pained*)   I've waited here since Thursday night. I've not slept, except for snatches in that chair, terrified I'd miss the phone ringing. After all that, you walk in here on Saturday morning and lie to me. (*Anger surfacing.*) Do you think I'm a child who can't face the truth? What trouble are you in? You simply wouldn't vanish on me. (*Sharply.*) This is about Derek, isn't it?

Jerome   No.

Penny   I walked around Ballymun yesterday describing him and Catherine. That pair of oddballs would stand out anywhere, yet no one recognised their description. Up and down stairs stinking of urine. You've spent years covering up for Derek, bailing him out of trouble. So what's he after dragging you into now?

Jerome   The sight of God.

Penny (*hurt*)   Don't mock me, please.

Jerome   Twice last night I woke to find the shape of nails in my palms. Only different now, made of beaten bronze, the heads chipped and buckled by hammer blows. I've never known such pain. I can't even scream. Then when I do scream the nails are gone but new wounds remain bleeding again.

Penny   Those men, they're holding Derek, aren't they? How much do you have to raise to get him released?

Jerome   You're not listening. On Thursday night I thought there was just the boy's presence there. But last night there was another presence. Outside, not in. A radiance pressing against the balcony window, hovering like a sword of light under the door, desperate to reach him.

Penny   What are you saying?

Jerome   Call it God, the Devil, call it what you will, but it was like a throbbing wave of heat. The very feel of it against the glass scorched my soul before it vanished and that terrible coldness returned, the sense of a child hanging from the neck alone.

Penny   Why can't you trust me with the truth, Jerome? How do I know some shower of thugs aren't going to burst through that door?

Jerome   I swear this has nothing to do with Derek.

Penny   Then are we in debt ourselves? Is it gambling . . . a moneylender?

Jerome   Derek's in England. I told you.

Penny   But you phoned from his flat? You offered to let me speak to him?

Jerome   He asked me to mind his flat. I was using it.

Penny   For what?

Jerome   All along God was pulling the strings.

Penny   I want to phone a doctor.

Jerome   These wounds follow their own pattern.

Penny   A psychiatrist. Clara gave me a name.

Jerome   I don't need a psychiatrist. I need you to believe me.

Penny   I'm phoning Clara now.

Jerome   No.

Penny   I need someone to confide in. I'm at my wits' end and you saunter in here spouting gibberish.

Jerome   Just for once in my life I'm trying to deal with the truth.

Penny   You always had a few kinks, but this is too much. What else were you doing in Derek's? Flogging yourself? Walking in bare feet over stones?

Jerome   I thought you were the one who believed in God?

Penny (*flustered*)   This isn't about God.

Jerome   I've never believed in anything. Da huffing and puffing at that organ. I knew it was a sham he joined in, so me and Derek could become respectable citizens. But all the time that crucified little Jew was lurking in his tabernacle. I'm petrified, because he's after breaking loose, like a big brother stalking me. Stop looking at me like I'm crazy . . . (*He steps forward.*) Penny?

Penny   You've nothing to atone for.

Jerome   You don't know me.

Penny (*stepping back*)   I know nothing that happened was
your fault. I know I've waited seven years for this to
come out in some madness, every feeling you kept bottled
up . . .

Jerome   This has nothing to do with Felicity. It has to do
with me, my compromises, my failures. We agreed not to talk
about Felicity.

Penny   Your life stopped that moment the doctors told you
her lungs weren't compatible with life. You pulled back into
yourself in a hard protective shell. Like you couldn't cope and
just blocked everything out.

Jerome   I stayed with you, throughout those eight days.

Penny   You were there but not with me. You'd switched off,
staring into that incubator like you were watching a dull film
on TV.

Jerome   We knew from the start there was no hope for her.
My first concern had to be for you.

Penny   So why all this talk of God now? Did you pray then,
even once for your own daughter?

Jerome   I did every practical thing I could, badgering
doctors, getting second opinions. If we could have flown her
anywhere I'd have found the money. If I could have given her
my own bloody lungs I would have. I could do nothing, just sit
and wait and watch you suffer.

Penny   And her. With every struggle for breath.

Jerome   And her.

Penny   And you as well.

Jerome   I didn't count.

Penny   You counted to me. You could have cried even,
you'd have felt better.

Jerome   I hated feeling so powerless. But we picked
ourselves up, we managed somehow to get by . . .

Penny   By you throwing yourself into work, the more calculating the better. That's no substitute for grief. Seven years ago you took a three-month break from the National Building agency to help Alex out. You're still with him, wasting away. Money, money, money, that's the only god you've had since then. Even these last months you're working late most nights till two in the morning. Look at yourself, Jerome, you're a breakdown waiting to happen. Maybe I'm to blame for refusing to recognise the signs. Even in your sleep you've been different, coiled up like you're afraid to touch me. It breaks my heart to see you like this. You need rest, to take stock of where you're going.

Jerome   I've been going nowhere, slipping from one lie to the next. Bathe my hands, please. They're aching.

Penny   Promise me you'll see the psychiatrist Clara knows. She can cover up for you in work. Alex will understand. (*She takes his hands.*) No one need ever be told. I didn't know what pain you're going through to do this to yourself. But you're safe now, you'll get the attention you need.

Jerome (*desperately*)   I need you to believe me.

Penny (*humouring him*)   If that's what you want. Let's bathe those wounds now.

Jerome (*sharply, pulling his hands back*)   It's not what I want. It's what happened. How can I stay if you don't believe me? I'll not be treated like a child. There was anger in your eyes when I came in. Now there's pity. That's why I couldn't come home before. I can't bear being pitied by you.

Penny   I believe we can make you well again.

Jerome   Believe that God led me to that flat.

Penny (*firmly*)   I'm no use to either of us by believing in fairy tales. Now give me your hands.

Jerome (*with low anger*)   Keep your hands to yourself. What a pity your Grandad died. He could have seen his worst suspicions confirmed. Papist son-in-law sees statues moving and the Blessed Virgin winking in the stars.

Penny   Holes in your hands are bad enough without chips on your shoulders. Stop it and show me those wounds.

Jerome   I can cope with the pain.

Penny   My nerves are shot. Now we gave up looking for miracles years ago.

Jerome   I can hardly remember who I was back then. It feels like I reinvented myself, piece by piece, shedding my skin as circumstances arose.

Penny   That's what people do, Jerome. It's called progress.

Jerome   My mother was for progress, sweeping us upwards and out. Unfortunately I seem to have taken an enormous step backwards. I have to pack some clothes.

Penny (*alarmed*)   Where are you going?

Jerome   Back to where I'm needed.

Penny   I need you. I'm your wife, for God's sake.

Jerome   You married someone else. Someone who died long ago. You don't know what I've become.

Penny   Maybe you didn't beg God, but I did, night after night, year after year. Do you think he listened? Do you think he heard? Do you think he bothered to lift his little finger to help us? Now why should he suddenly choose the likes of you for anything?

Jerome   I wish I knew.

Penny   You cannot go off like this.

Jerome   Leave your family and follow me, Jesus said.

Penny   He said it to fishermen without mortgages. What kind of God drives a husband and wife apart? It wasn't my fault that Felicity died. Why are you punishing me now?

Jerome   How can I live with you, Penny, when I can't even live with myself? I don't know what's real anymore.

Penny (*blocking his way*)   I'm real, our marriage is real. My loneliness without you is real.

Jerome   I'm sorry. I have to go.

Penny   Sorry isn't enough. This is cowardice. Copping out on real life.

Jerome   For years I've taken the easy route. I didn't choose this path, but I'm not turning back.

Penny (*bitterly*)   Go on then. Because only cowards hide behind God and, for all your talk, I know you don't even have one to hide behind.

Jerome *exits over her line.* **Penny** *looks after him, then follows.*

Scene Two

Rita *enters in silence, top stage right, and hovers, waiting for* **Jerome**. **Jerome** *enters front stage left with a travel bag and reluctantly stops as he spots the* **Caretaker** *entering from front stage right.*

Caretaker   The bold man himself, Derek. I bet when John Stiles tried his yuppie integration experiment he didn't think it would have such an immediate effect.

Jerome   What are you talking about?

Caretaker (*indicates* **Rita**)   Disciples queuing for you already. (*Looks at* **Jerome**'s *unkempt appearance.*) You're going native on us. How about a few designer pockmarks in the veins?

Jerome   I'll dress any way I like.

Caretaker   You can roll in the muck, pal, they still won't accept you here.

Jerome   What have you got against me?

Caretaker (*looks around*)   I remember these towers before anybody moved in. We thought they were the bee's knees. Innocent times, that shit Blaney and Haughey swanning out in their mohair suits and braces. None of us knew what lay ahead.

Jerome   We rarely do.

Caretaker   Is Catherine not with you again today or those kids of hers?

Jerome   No. Now let me pass, please.

Caretaker   Of course, they're not really yours, John Stiles said, an acquired possession. You must like acquiring things. I mean overnight you've acquired quite a reputation here. Though anyone who lives in that flat does.

Jerome   Why?

Caretaker   You tell me.

Jerome   Did you know the boy who died there?

Caretaker   His father had the only job on that landing. You'd think they'd be happy. (*He looks up.*) His mother fell from the balcony there. When people fall, suicide is always mentioned. I don't believe it though, no matter what problems she had. She never struck me as having many, except the husband she brought home from Coventry. She should have gone on back to Cork where she knew people. What's the thrill some men get from violence? You'd hear him shouting, like he wanted to be overheard. And the boy in between them, begging him to stop.

Jerome   Are you saying she was pushed?

Caretaker   I'm saying she loved her son. Mothers rarely quit when they love their sons.

Jerome   What did the police say?

Caretaker   Jumpers are five-day wonders. I could draw a map down here of all the spots where blood got washed away. The young lad was alone a lot after she died. You'd hear him singing pop songs to himself, acting out fantasies with air guitars. He lived in his head mainly, no real pals. People gave his Da a wide berth too. Nothing was ever proven, but let's just say that, even when the pub was packed, he drank with empty seats around him. Being English didn't help, made him seem an outsider anyway. Maybe he was innocent, but enough people decided to be his judge and jury so that by the end pills and booze were his only friends. I was there the morning it happened, trying to get the lifts fixed. The boy came running out, saying he couldn't wake his Da. We phoned an ambulance. There was no one else to call, he didn't seem to have relatives, except for some number in Cork that seemed to have been disconnected. We shouldn't have left him alone, even for a minute. God knows, it didn't take much longer, a length of twine so thin you'd swear it would snap. You torture yourself with guilt afterwards. (*He looks down.*) What happened your hands?

Jerome   An accident.

Caretaker   Sounded more like an attack according to Mrs McCormack in the flat below you. Screams carry. You've become our local curiosity. People are taking bets on how long you'll last. Eleven months is the longest anyone stuck that flat, a young Galway woman with a baby. One night is the shortest, a whole family from Finglas found outside huddled on the stairway. But he never physically hurt anyone before.

Jerome   If I was attacked by local yobs it's my own business.

Caretaker   They fled through the locked door, did they? Carrying off your girlfriend and kids?

Jerome   The rent is paid up. What more do you want?

Caretaker   Paid by whom for whom? I'd a drink with John Stiles last night. He described you as a scrawny fuck with a ponytail, a ringer for the guy who told me he was off to England and to stuff the flat. There's a clause about sub-letting, so if you're not Derek Furlong then I want you out of there.

Jerome   What difference is it to you?

Caretaker   Maybe I feel guilty still about leaving the boy alone. I want his flat boarded up until they tear this blasted tower down.

Jerome   Derek will be home in a few weeks with his tail between his legs. He'll need it then. I'm his brother.

Caretaker   Are you now? (*Points towards* **Rita**.) Rita Boyle claims she met you in hospital. Stories spread.

Jerome   She had no right to talk.

Caretaker   Show me your hands so. Tell me her stories are lies.

Jerome   You wouldn't believe me.

Caretaker   I'd believe anything about that flat. Noises, even when the place is boarded up. Boxes thrown against walls, boxes no one person could lift, certainly no boy his age.

Jerome   If there is a ghost, how do you know it's him?

Caretaker   Whenever another child is there he's more peaceful. Less disturbances at night, sometimes none for weeks. He's attached to babies, protective even. All you might get is soft toys tossed around a cot. The woman who stayed for eleven months said that by the end she'd learnt not to mind him. When the room went cold she'd know he was here but she'd stopped being frightened. She might have stayed on if her baby wasn't thrown from its cot one night. Next day she asked me to dismantle the cot. I was in the corridor when I looked back. I saw a boy in a blue mortuary shroud, cowering like he knew he'd done something wrong. Just for a second, as if afraid somebody would strike him. Then the image was gone.

Jerome   I didn't know it was a mortuary shroud.

Caretaker   So you have seen him too?

Jerome   I never believed in ghosts before.

Caretaker   Nor did I, despite the banging. I thought it was a scam, people faking to get shifted to better homes. Since then . . . (*He lets the sentence trail away.*) The woman moved back to Galway. The day she took the curtains down that flat erupted. Glass shattering, pictures thrown off every wall. I suppose he couldn't take the idea of being abandoned again. Now I want that flat empty and his spirit undisturbed. If your brother wants to live there he needs to turn up in person to take possession. John Stiles didn't sound too keen on it being sub-let as a knocking shop for someone with a Guinness Mahon Bank account.

Jerome   What if that boy wants something from me?

Caretaker (*less officious*)   For God's sake, man, look at yourself. You don't know what you're dealing with. Now just go and leave his ghost alone, for his sake and your own.

The **Caretaker** *exits and* **Jerome** *turns to stare towards* **Rita***, who sees him and rises nervously as he approaches her.*

Rita (*tentatively*)   Mister?

Jerome   What do you want?

Rita   Just to talk.

Jerome   You've done enough talking already.

Rita   What do you mean?

Jerome   I feel like a circus freak. You'd no right to tell strangers about me.

Rita   You told me.

Jerome   I was confused.

Rita   Have your hands stopped bleeding?

Jerome   My hands are my own concern.

Rita   Don't be falling out with me. Especially when I've come to ask a favour.

Jerome   I have no money. My wife, I left her my credit cards, everything.

Rita (*deeply insulted*)   Did I ask for money? Did I mention money? Did I come here begging, did I? I've worked my whole life, Mister, from the age of thirteen. Laundries, packing lines, gutting fish out beyond Finglas. Maybe not clean jobs like yours, but I've owed nobody nothing, no loan man, no tick at the shops. I've paid my way and reared my children to do the same. I thought you were chosen by God, but you're not. I don't know what you are, but don't you try and make me feel cheap.

She turns away, insulted.

Jerome   Wait, please, I'm sorry. (*She turns.*) My life has been turned upside-down. Nobody believes what's happened to me. I don't know what to do.

Rita   I believe. God has chosen you.

Jerome   Why?

Rita   He chose fishermen and labourers, people who could never explain why He chose them. Don't you see? We're all parts of the one jigsaw and only He sees the whole picture.

Jerome   Then what do I do with these stupid wounds?

Rita   Heal.

Jerome   What?

Rita   Look around you, Mister. If ever a healer was needed then here and now is the place.

Jerome   I can't heal anyone.

Rita   No. But God can . . . through you.

Jerome   That's crazy talk.

Rita   How do you know what powers are in those wounds?

Jerome   I don't want to even hear this.

Rita   You can't run away from it, Mister. You don't know what you can do till you try. (*Beat.*) I asked you to pray for my granddaughter.

Jerome   I've forgotten her name, I'm sorry.

Rita   Why do you think we met? I'd been praying for a sign in the hospital chapel, for some glimmer of hope, then suddenly there you were in the waiting room. You even said yourself you'd tried to walk home and the pain in your wounds forced you back. She's fading, Mister, running out of time. The doctors say that unless a donor is found in the next few days there's no hope. From them at least. But maybe not from you.

Jerome (*alarmed*)   What can I do, pray that other child dies? I can't help, I swear.

Rita   Enough children have died. Can't you see? When you said you were in that flat I knew why God had sent you. A boy died there, needlessly, a life wasted. Maybe this is God's way of making sense of his death, by sending you to me. A life for a life. Maybe some other child doesn't have to die to save Jacinta.

Jerome   What do you mean?

Rita   God works in ways we can't understand, the things he makes us endure. Will you not just try to pray over her? Maybe her lungs might strengthen, even for a few weeks. You could touch her with the wounds that Our Lord made in your palms. You're suffering pain, Mister, I see it in your eyes. But God makes nobody suffer needlessly. There has to be a purpose behind those wounds. I'm begging you. Have you any idea what it's like to see a child struggle to breathe, to see the future being snuffed out before your eyes?

Jerome   I'm scared of going back there.

Rita (*disgusted*)   You're too proud to pray over a sick child, you mean. Scared of hospitals! Wouldn't life be great, if that was all we had to be scared of?

Jerome   Maybe I'm scared of failing you. I've no powers. I can't just take the weight of your hopes in my hands.

Rita   My granddaughter's dying, Mister, and all I'm hearing is about you being scared. Isn't it better to have failed than to have sat on your arse in life and done nothing?

Jerome (*beat*)   What is it that you want me to do?

Rita   Give me half an hour of your time.

Jerome   Then you'll leave me alone? And tell no one else, even if by some quirk she is cured.

Rita   You can walk away from here, Mister, and keep going. A hundred miles, a thousand, but you'll never walk away from your destiny if that is what God has chosen for you.

Rita *exits and* **Jerome** *follows her.*

Scene Three

The **Doctor** *and a* **Nurse** *wheel a hospital bed on to the centre of the stage, in which an unseen child lies with a breathing mask over her face. She is attached to a ventilator, from which comes the heavy rasp of laboured breathing. They park the bed and exit.* **Rita** *leads* **Jerome** *on-stage and towards the bed. He hesitates, then stands at her shoulder, staring down in silence for a moment.*

Jerome (*softly*)   Oh my God. (*To* **Rita**.) What do I do?

Rita   I don't know, Mister. Pray. Lay your hands on her. People in the tower offered to raise money to fly her to Lourdes, but sure the trip would kill her. A right little tomboy she was once. (*She glances behind.*) Quickly, while she's asleep. Before the nurses come back.

Jerome (*nervously*)   I don't know what to say.

Rita   She's dying before your eyes. God has chosen you, man, now for pity's sake, will you not just pray?

Jerome (*blessing himself awkwardly*)   'Our father, who art in heaven . . .'

Rita (*prompting as he falters*)   'Hallowed . . .'

Jerome   'Hallowed be Thy name. Thy Kingdom come, Thy, Thy . . .'

Rita   'Will be done . . .' The nurses will be here soon.

Jerome (*rattled*)   I'm sorry, it's been a long time. (*Looks at*

Rita.) Please, leave me alone with her.

Rita   You promise to anoint her forehead with blood.

Jerome (*jittery*)   I promise. Now please . . .

Rita *looks down, blesses herself, then retreats into the shadows.*
Jerome, *alone in the light around the bed, touches the child's unseen face.*

Jerome (*to the child*)   You can't hear me, can you? Drugged into sleep. (*Looks heavenward.*) Can you? On your throne or wherever you sit to pretend you watch over us? Lord, I've not asked you for much in this life. Maybe if I had then at times things might have been different, I don't know. I know nothing, except that you've sent me needless, ridiculous pain. But I'll bear it and more, as much public ridicule as you wish to heap on me. I'll bear anything if it has a purpose, so let its purpose be in this child. What earthly sense is there in bringing another child into the world to have her die like this? Just how many deaths are needed to satisfy your blood lust? I mean I've seen your justice and mercy, and it left me no great fan of your games. I'm forty, Lord. I've had my shot at living and I've chickened out, all my life taking the easy paths, making such a balls of everything that I hardly recognise myself anymore. So just give me this one chance to atone. Give me this girl's suffering. Strike me dead or dumb or crippled if you wish, just let her breathing come easy. You like sacrifices in your games, well here I'm making them. I'm a blunt man, Lord, not into prayer. You're holding all the cards, five bloody aces. You're winning hands down, so how about blinking just once, show one scrap of mercy. You owe me one, you bastard, bringing me back here, making me relive every memory. So okay, you've had your joke, now here's the deal. I take these bandages off. (*He begins to do so.*) I anoint her face with blood from the wounds you've made. Redouble the pain if you like, triple it, only let my suffering have some purpose. I've asked nothing from you before, I've borne grief my own way. I've seen my daughter struggle into this world, then curl up into a small stiff ball. A white coffin carried on a black day, just the weight of feathers, of emptiness. (*He dips his finger in his* *wound and touches the girl's face.*) I'll count to three, Lord, and let your will be done. If you know the meaning of pity in that Sacred Heart of yours, then just give this child the mercy that you withheld from mine.

Jerome *stands back, gazing intently down at the bed. The* **Doctor** *re-enters, surprised to find him there and approaches the bed. He stares down as the* **Nurse** *appears in the shadows.*

Doctor (*softly*)   Oh, my God almighty! Good Sweet Jesus.

His voice brings **Rita** *in from the shadows.*

Doctor (*wonder-struck*)   What have you done to the girl? What are you after doing?

Rita *looks down and blesses herself.*

Doctor (*shock giving way to anger*)   Blood smeared all over her face! What sort of perverted bastard are you? Who let you in here? You're the chap who ran out of casualty on Thursday night . . . Furlong, isn't it? I should have phoned the police then. Cover up those hands. Don't tell me you're still going around with them like that? This child is sick. (*To* **Rita**.) We found this lunatic leaning over your granddaughter, Mrs Boyle, do you want us to phone the police?

Rita   No.

Doctor (*to* **Jerome**)   Get the hell out of here before she changes her mind, and get those hands seen to properly, for God's sake.

Jerome (*to* **Rita**)   I'm sorry. If I could take her pain I would.

Doctor (*surprised, to* **Rita**)   Is this man with you?

Rita (*quietly*)   I don't know who he is or what he thinks he's doing here.

Jerome *looks at* **Rita** *who looks away. He takes a last look at the child and flees. The* **Doctor** *and* **Nurse** *wheel the bed off, while* **Rita** *silently watches, then follows.*

Scene Four

Lights come up in the flat as **Jerome** *enters, his body twisted in fury. He kicks out at a box in anger and self-disgust.*

Jerome   Play Jesus my bollix! He can't even play his fucking self. If some bastarding God wants you then he can come for you himself, because I'm sick of being his plaything. (*Turns and looks around.*) Are you listening, poltergeist, zombie, scared shitless ghost? You want a show of pyrotechnics, I'll give you one. (*He kicks over a box.*) You want to throw boxes, I'll throw boxes. Want to scatter nails? (*He picks up the bag of nails and throws them towards the wing.*) I'll scatter nails for you. You needn't think such tricks can keep me here just because you're scared of the dark on your own. I'm walking out, back to whatever life I have left.

Jerome *stops suddenly, as if he has bumped into something. He puts his hand out, touching an unseen shape hanging before him, which may be suggested by a subtle lighting change.*

Jerome (*terrified*)   So cold . . . like ice . . . hanging there, swaying . . . I can't see you, can't see nothing . . . just feel your shape . . . (*His hands outline the shape of a body.*) What am I supposed to do? Get a chair and cut you down? I've passed this spot a hundred times before without feeling . . . I'm going crazy, crazy . . .

Clara *enters the flat on this last word.*

Clara (*calling softly*)   Jerome?

Jerome (*looks around, startled*)   Clara? Is that you?

Clara   The door was open.

Jerome *steps back, with the unseen body between* **Clara** *and himself.*

Jerome (*frightened*)   Walk over to me . . . here . . . please. (**Clara** *begins to walk, slightly off-line.*) No, to your left, now straight ahead.

Clara (*reaching the spot where the unseen body hangs*)   What's going on, Jerome?

Jerome   Stop. Put your hands out, just there.

Clara   You're making me nervous.

Jerome   Do you feel anything?

Clara   I feel you're cracking up.

Jerome   Why have you come?

Clara   Penny phoned after you left this morning. She was crying so much that at first I thought you'd told her.

Jerome   Maybe I should have.

Clara   Why cause unnecessary suffering over something that's over? Nobody wants the full truth. That's how we survive, by parcelling off bits of our lives.

Jerome   Maybe we need to face the truth to grow.

Clara   You've done all your growing, Jerome. After forty it's fading eyesight, rotting teeth, organs struggling to do what came natural once. Some men take up gardening, more chase prostitutes, the scared ones find God. I should know, my father did all three.

Jerome   You never mentioned him before.

Clara   You never asked, did you? I grew up in a house anyone would envy, white pillars, electronic gates, a chauffeur taking me to school.

Jerome   You always struck me as rich.

Clara   We were poor, dirt poor. Maybe not in the real world, he earned more than a bus driver I suppose, but behind those gates we were the poorest thing that ever lived. Everybody else's job description was well defined, it took me until I was eleven to figure out what Daddy did. He was a facilitator, the man with no eyes who didn't exist. He worked for Hugh Jeffers.

Jerome   The plastics magnate whose plane crashed?

Clara   We lived in so that Daddy could be around at night. Hugh Jeffers liked to bring girls home, secretaries I suppose and bright young wanabees looking like schoolgirls getting out of his limo. The fattest ugliest man with hairdye running on his collar after he showered with them. Daddy was vital. It was a big house in Dalkey, rambling corridors. They must have thought he'd eyes in the back of his head, but Daddy would have me positioned, sitting up half the night on landings sometimes. It wasn't that Mrs Jeffers didn't know, the dogs on the street knew. It was to ensure that their paths didn't cross, later on when she brought her toyboys home through the back corridor.

Jerome   You were only a child then.

Clara   It's how the world works. I've been lucky, I never had illusions to shatter. You may get to see into a lot of bright rooms along the corridor but you always wind up sitting in the dark alone.

Jerome   Life isn't like that.

Clara   How can you say that after what we've done?

Jerome   Things were meant to turn out different. Penny and I . . . we had hopes once.

Clara   It's always two a.m. somewhere and somebody's footsteps are creeping away. The secret is to leave them before they leave you. Tell me that what I'm about to do is wrong.

Jerome   What is it?

Clara   You and Alex, you're Mickey Mouse operators really, but I liked you both. I liked the way you used to argue about whose turn it was to make the coffee and steal each other's Polo mints. You had all the moves and the groves, but, Jesus, were you playing in one small league. Still you taught me the rules of how to operate.

Jerome   It seems a long time ago.

Clara   Tell me I should stay with your agency, that I shouldn't accept the Silverskin offer.

Jerome   What offer?

Clara   Look after number one first, you always said. I can do a deal for myself that even you'd be proud of, so why can't I feel good about it?

Jerome   You can sell the Dracula pitch to Silverskin?

Clara   I can sell myself. You're losing the Silverskin account. The Peters Agency is getting it. Silverskin have been spinning you along to get a better deal. They think Dracula is your first original concept in years.

Jerome   They told Alex this?

Clara   Alex introduced Dracula as my concept. They phoned me at home and said they'd make it a condition of the Peters contract that I'm offered a position working on their account.

Jerome   That's good news for you.

Clara   Is it? They say other clients are leaving too, it's like a house of cards collapsing around you. Tell me I should stay.

Jerome   Why?

Clara   Because you want me to. Because it's the decent thing. Out of loyalty. Tell me I've been wrong all my life, that it's not simply a fuck or be fucked world. Tell me that life doesn't have to be built on top of a heap of petty betrayals.

Jerome   I'm no one to talk. You should go, get ahead, do well for yourself.

Clara   I was never your mistress, Jerome. Didn't you notice? I was your lover. Don't ask me why I loved you, I never even got to know you. You were like a box of contradictions, every time I opened it somebody else popped up, lying to themselves.

Jerome   You've always known where you're going. I never did.

Clara   Go back to Penny. I feel bad about it now, whereas before I felt that if you didn't care then why should I? I simply wanted what I wanted and everything I'd ever learnt, from you, from my father, from anyone else, told me it was right to go for it, to grab from life whatever you could. I even had plans, in a year or two, to have a child from you. When I got settled in a proper job, independent, financially secure. I mean I know that you and Penny have no interest in kids, and I wouldn't have let you be involved or even told you who the father was, but I'd have liked a child by you to raise in my own way, without that family shite we all had to go through.

Jerome   You'll need to find another donor now I'm afraid.

Clara   End this delusion, Jerome, for my sake. I never asked for anything before, but I don't like leaving you here like this. You looked so terrified when I came in.

Jerome's *hands pass through the unseen shape, which he finds is gone.*

Jerome (*to himself*)   There's nothing here . . . nothing. (*Looks at* **Clara**.) I should never have tried cocaine. It flipped me. That's all there was to it. You walk away, keep going.

Clara   Religion is a dangerous thing. I'm glad we did French and computers instead. We never felt the need to tie ourselves up in chains. (*Awkward beat.*) You should see somebody, a priest or someone. Things like that don't happen, they're only metaphors.

Jerome (*to himself again*)   Betrayal, it's in my blood . . . the coward's way . . . to anyone who ever needed me.

Clara   What?

Jerome   You just go on, eh?

Clara   Let me at least drive you to Malahide.

Jerome   I'll be fine.

Clara   You were right about Derek, by the way. He phoned, hoping you'd send the fare home. It seems the gallery in London expected Catherine to pay them up front, some sort of vanity showcase in an old warehouse. They're getting the boat back. I couriered the money from petty cash.

Jerome   That pair drive me daft.

Clara   Why bother with him so?

Jerome   I happen to love the stupid fucker and I envy him
too. I got six straight As in my Leaving Cert, did I ever tell you
that? And a B honour in maths. My mother, she put her hand
on my shoulder, she sighed. You could feel decades of
disappointment in that sigh. All she could say was 'what a
terrible pity about your maths.'

Clara   How did Derek do?

Jerome   Everyone thought it wonderful when he strung five
passes together and one C honour in French. It wasn't
important, you see, he'd a big brother who was going to
redeem the family. He even looks the spit of Da, forever
failing, forever chasing after the next stupid dream.

Clara (*mockingly*)   'Carlow's ivory-tinkling dentist.'

Jerome   Can you play a single note?

Clara   No.

Jerome   Well my Da could, even with a tremble in his
hands he could make music, even when he shook so much he
could hardly hold a knife and fork he kept plugging on. So
don't you mock him.

Clara (*with quiet patience, as if to a child*)   It's hard to stop,
Jerome. Ever since I've known you, you mocked him, yourself
and every single thing you were too frightened to admit you
cared about. (*Beat.*) I left some personal things in the office,
you might courier them out to me.

Clara *walks off, leaving him alone as lights fade to blackout.*

Scene Five

Light rises, suggesting morning as **Jerome** *confronts a middle-aged*
Priest *in a jumper and casual leather jacket who has entered the*
flat.

Priest   Forgive the early call, I probably should have booked, especially on Easter Sunday morning. Your fame goes before you, the Jesus of Ballymun, almost curer of sick children, turner of cider into wine.

Jerome   Who the hell are you?

Priest   Eamonn Maguire. Father. I received a visitation from a well-dressed lady, concerned for your mental welfare. She stood in the presbytery, like she'd stepped into dog poo, and declined to give a name. Your wife?

Jerome   Mistress. Ex.

Priest   Very posh. I'm impressed.

Jerome   I didn't invite you here.

Priest   Perhaps curiosity got the better of me or I needed some light relief. I've enough cares in the real world with kids sleeping in cardboard boxes and selling their bodies for a fix. Maybe I needed a gawk at the yuppie Matt Talbot. Personally I'm a 'Biffo' myself: A Big, Ignorant Fucker From Offaly. Toss us out a few greyhounds mauling a live hare and we're happy as pigs in shite in Offaly. We haven't discovered sophisticated entertainments like sticking holes in our hands. However I'm as liberal as the next man, so go ahead. I mean there are men on the Internet boasting about sticking chains through their foreskins so their lovers can take them out for walkies. We're pretty unshockable, us priests, these days, which – considering what some of the men I trained with got up to – is hardly surprising. But just one word of advice, don't condescend to descend on us here from some posh suburb and expect people to be impressed.

Jerome   I want nothing to do with your sort.

Priest   I rather felt we wouldn't be exclusive enough all right. God needs to call you for a personal appointment first.

Jerome   He didn't call. I've had no say in this, do you understand?

Priest   I understand that when I was a child we'd whole legions of sins. Now that sin has evaporated we're stuck with guilt instead. For your own sake, stick whatever guilt is driving you back into your pocket before you're eaten alive here.

Jerome   Is that the sermon over?

Priest   No. There was one time Saint Peter got bored on the gates of paradise and asked Jesus to do bouncer. A little old man in the queue announced that he was a humble village carpenter there in search for his one and only son, a tall young man with holes in his hands and feet. Jesus put out his hands and cried 'Daddy'. The old man ran to him, crying 'Picinocco'. Look at yourself, Mr Furlong. You make a better Picinocco than a Jesus, I'm afraid.

Jerome   How did you get to be this cynical?

Priest   It's a fringe benefit from queuing with people, day after day. You realise that helping people involves more than tossing a few flecks of blood over a sick girl and praying that she recovers.

Jerome   I shouldn't have gone near that hospital. The woman was desperate, clinging to any hope.

Priest   Desperate people do.

Jerome   I got swept along, stupidly seeing myself making the lame walk and the blind see.

Priest   Hope is an infectious disease. You tread dangerously when you meddle with it.

Jerome   Your God meddled with me. I'm a busy man, with no time for hoaxes.

Priest   Maybe God hasn't either.

Jerome   Then who does? I'm scared shitless and my palms ache. Did you know the family who lived here?

Priest   The husband rarely welcomed callers.

Jerome   Have you known tenants here since?

Priest   Nobody stays long enough.

Jerome   Last night I woke and the boy appeared to me, for the third time, his head loping to one side, his neck broken. His mouth opened, like he was trying to speak, like thousand of words were choked inside him. Then through the window behind him I heard a whisper, 'suffer for me, carry me to him'. The boy disappeared and I could see a blurred shape pressed against the window, like a starfish with six fins that gradually became wings. One above and one below, two at the side beating through the air and two turned inwards to hold the shape of a crucifix. All the coldness evaporated from this room, except in that spot where I knew the boy's invisible figure hung. Everywhere else felt alive with electricity. I was petrified, in the presence of something overwhelming. It wanted something from me, but I didn't know what to do. Then suddenly this pain burst through my palms again.

Priest   I expected someone different, a deranged zealot. I don't know what to say to you.

Jerome   Sometimes the boy is a distant presence, like an echo left behind. Other times I feel him like a cold breath on my neck. Sometimes my legs shake, like jelly turning to ice. He's my jailer, watching me. Sometimes he throws objects, plays stupid games, I feel his rage.

Priest   Three times I was asked to say Mass here. If his spirit is trapped here then I haven't the power to release it.

Jerome   Sometimes in the dark I feel other presences waiting for him to join them. Eyes at the window, eyes in every knot and whorl of wood.

Priest   People often imagine they see visions. They're rare but not uncommon, like the number thirty-six bus around here.

Jerome   Are you saying you don't believe me?

Priest   I'm saying that I can't afford to believe you. The last thing I need here are miracles. They're a nuisance, freak show curiosities. I don't need statues weeping blood or apostles' faces in wardrobe doors. And I definitely don't need middle-aged executives meddling with forces they know nothing about, forces I've seen destroy men who've spent their lives studying them. I'm sorry, but what I need is a hostel for homeless boys, a stable for stray horses, schools for traveller children. I need a network of bogus addresses outside this area so that school-leavers can get called for job interviews. I need a station wagon that isn't clapped out. Personally (if you're talking to God) I'd like to own a small alarm clock radio for more than a week without it being stolen. I need people looking up to demand their rights, not down on their knees before some mutilation.

Jerome   I never asked for anyone's attention.

Priest   You won't have to. You'll be amazed how desperate people are to believe in something. Do you honestly think you can walk around with stigmata and not have people besieging you and coming away disappointed?

Jerome   Do you not think I've tried to stem these wounds?

Priest   I'm a simple man. I just think you'd be safer among your own kind.

Jerome   You mean I should run away, like everyone else, from the pain in this flat.

Priest   It's not your pain. Do you really imagine you can heal him?

Jerome   Maybe I can heal myself.

Priest   You're a freak. People are frightened of freaks and no one likes being frightened. I can't protect you here. It's not like years ago with pulpits and big sticks.

Jerome   I'll take my chances.

Priest   You'll need them.

Jerome   Pray for me sometime.

Priest   God doesn't take my calls. You pray for me. He might just listen.

Jerome *nods and the* **Priest** *turns and exits. Blackout.*

Scene Six

Light comes up as **Jerome** *leads* **Penny** *into the flat.*

Jerome   You found the flat.

Penny   Surprisingly easily. Girls at a bus stop, giggling. (*Forced accent.*) 'You mean the geezer who thinks he's Jesus.'

Jerome   I'm sorry. You must find the ridicule embarrassing.

Penny   I've stood outside, waiting for you all afternoon. I didn't know if you were at home waiting for me.

Jerome   I wish to God I could be.

Penny   Who are you running from? Me or yourself or what we've become?

Jerome   I've always loved you. Badly, blindly, even when you felt like a ragdoll I was tearing apart in my hands.

Penny   Why?

Jerome   What?

Penny   I never knew why you loved me. I used to say 'do you still love me?' and you'd say 'yes' and when I'd ask again you'd get annoyed. I felt insecure. I'd look at myself and could never figure out why.

Jerome   I loved your stillness, your white Protestant breasts.

Penny   Don't mock.

Jerome   I'm not. That's how I saw them. As exotic somehow, foreign, different to taste, different to touch. That word fitted everything about you. Within a week I knew I wanted to marry you.

Penny   I wanted to be loved for myself.

Jerome   I did, but being who you were helped to make you special. As a kid I used to sneak into the porch of the Protestant church and look in at the polished pews and neat piles of bibles and those stone tablets inscribed to the fallen in the Great War. I loved its sense of difference. Maybe our God spoke Latin, but your God spoke French and was a man of the world.

Penny   It was nothing like that.

Jerome   That's how it seemed to an outsider. No babies crying. No drunk playing the organ, fuelled by failed hopes and black coffee. No mother forever urging you to build up the facade, brick by brick, that we were different, better than what we'd once been. It was just stiff-faced old ladies in Morris Minors.

Penny   A lost tribe looking down on a vanished world.

Jerome   These last seven years I've been more lost than they ever were.

Penny   You always knew what you wanted.

Jerome   I wanted to belong somewhere else, to walk in from that porch and leave all the petty responsibilities and weight of my parents' hopes behind. I wanted to be someone special like you are. From the day we met I wanted your goodness. It seemed that all my life I'd been waiting to meet you. Your skin, your hair, the way you never even knew how special you were. That tiny bedsit your father owned in Fitzwilliam Square. I used to lie curled up against you in the single bed and watch you sleeping. I'd never felt such a sense of purpose. I was living my own dreams now. I'd have killed gladly for you and for any child that came from your womb. You didn't just smell of soap and sex, you smelt of sins forgiven and redemption.

Penny   What do I smell of now?

Jerome   I lost my sense of smell when Felicity died. Suddenly the whole world tasted of cardboard.

Penny   You never even cried.

Jerome   When I tried to all the tears were gone. Nothing left inside me but an arid desert where coyotes and prairie dogs roamed. That's the most shocking thing about these wounds. They're like wells springing up through the barren sand. I deserve this pain multiplied by a hundred times.

Penny   Felicity died because her lungs weren't compatible with life. There was nothing you could have done.

Jerome   Maybe there's something I can do now.

Penny   That's crazy talk.

Jerome   Is it? Where is her soul? What if she's lost and frightened like the boy in this flat? Why could I never give you a child again? Why? Why?

Penny   You know why. You know we tried.

Jerome   I did it once. The only miracle in my life, so why not again? Why?

Penny   Jerome . . . ?

Jerome   Yesterday . . . it was sheer madness . . . I honestly thought I could cure a sick child, that I could trade my pain off as like a down payment on her life. It was in that same fucking hospital we sat in day after day. I'd sworn never to go near it again. But God was sparing me nothing from his repertoire of tricks. Jesus falls, Jesus is whipped, Jesus is crowned with thorns.

Penny   You're not Jesus.

Jerome   No. I'm the hermit forced out of hiding in my cave in the mountains to deal with all the shit and the squalor I'd run away from. I've been up in Glasnevin cemetery all afternoon, the little angel's plot.

Penny   You'd always refuse to even come in the gates there with me.

Jerome   I simply couldn't face it or face you crying there.

All the names and ages on the headstones – counted not in years, but in weeks and days – and the toys left, cars and teddies, the stupid meaningless birthday cards. They still have Felicity's name misspelt, remember how we told them to correct it. The bastards never carved her right name on.

Penny   Is her plot full now?

Jerome   Two girls and a boy buried after her. Their parents go a lot by the look of it. I felt closer to her there today than when she lay in that incubator.

Penny   Nothing you're putting yourself through here can bring her back.

Jerome   Maybe it will let her go.

Penny   What do you mean?

Jerome   Maybe she'll be free of us if I can only free this boy's spirit.

Penny   That's a lot of maybes. Look at the state of you, you always kept yourself so neat. Yet the funny thing is you look so alive, like the first time we met. I have the car parked below.

Jerome   I can't go home yet.

Penny   No, but I can stay.

Jerome (*surprised*)   What? You can't stay here. You'd hate this place.

Penny   If this is what you want, what you need to do, then can't you see that I'm willing to share it too?

Jerome   This tower block is dangerous. You weren't reared to live here.

Penny   I wasn't reared in a glass case either, you just put me in one. I'm capable of living anywhere, once I'm with the man I love. I was happy in that bedsit in Fitzwilliam Square, remember? I never asked for a big house in Malahide, you insisted on giving me one.

Jerome   I wanted to give you the things you were used to.

Penny   I was used to drafty corridors, to leaking roofs and rattling windows, the cheapest toilet paper cutting the backside off me in winter. Did you never look at my grandfather's house collapsing around his ears? The old fool selling off land in bits and bobs, seeing it rezoned and suddenly worth thousands of pounds more, too stand-offish to bribe a few councillors himself and make a killing. All I ever wanted was you. I don't honestly know what is wrong with your hands. But if this flat is where you want to be then it's good enough for me.

Jerome   I'll not be pitied or treated like I'm mad.

Penny   If you're mad, then maybe that's what I've been for seven years too. How do you know what I might believe in, when we never talk? What things I've seen and heard? How for years in our house alone I've heard a baby crying, stumbling from one empty room to the next searching for a trace of her. That I've woken at night with such an ache in my breasts, I've felt milk welling up inside them, the nipples raw like they'd been greedily sucked. I've been haunted by more dreams and demons than you'll ever know. I felt things I could never tell you because I know you'd just mock them, like you've mocked everything. So don't you tell me now what I may or may not believe in.

Jerome   You never said a word.

Penny   What was the point in talking to a stranger? Do you not think I've been tortured with thoughts of where Felicity's soul is? We made her between us, nine months in my womb, eight days in an incubator. Let nobody try to tell me that her spirit disappeared in one last dying breath. I know all about God, because I cursed him with every name under the sun. I cursed him like you never knew I could curse, because you men curse for bravado, but we women really mean it. You never saw the paintings up in our attic, distorted forms streaked with my own blood that I've cursed every month, demons coming alive on canvas soaked with paint and matted with blood, then ripped apart with my nails. All you ever saw were watercolours because that is all I let you see, because I knew it was all you were able to cope with.

Jerome   Penny . . . please . . .

Penny   Penny no please anymore. Penny at home, Penny
for no thoughts of her own. Penny who cursed you too that
your cock couldn't pass muster. All the complicated answers
from the specialists, always holding out the vague hope of
another fluke, but all the time your balls were simply too
small.

Jerome   That wasn't my fault.

Penny   Maybe not, but there were nights when I'd have
fucked anything, I'd have climbed up on the fucking tomcat if
it could have got us our daughter back.

Jerome   Don't curse.

Penny   I'll curse just fine. (*Sings.*) 'Hitler had only one big
ball, Jerome had two but very small . . .'

Jerome   Stop it.

Penny   Balls, cunt, cock. Does it frighten you that I'm not a
piece of Protestant bone china stoically coping with her
husband's mania? Don't tell me that I can't cope with living in
Ballymun, because we haven't been living for years, Jerome.
We've suffered in silence till we cracked apart. Now this flat is
as good as anywhere to start again from scratch. It doesn't
matter a damn to me whether those holes were made by the
Holy Ghost or a Black 'n Decker. I just know that you're in
pain and so am I. Maybe at least here we can share that
openly. I want to be held by you and cry instead of always
crying behind your back. I want to help you, Jerome, because
you're all I have left to live for.

Jerome   You don't know who I've become, what things I've
done.

Penny   I know more than maybe you know about yourself.
I know when you think I'm asleep and you lie awake for
hours. I know the silence you sit in, drinking brandy alone at
night.

Jerome   There are other things you don't know.

Penny   What things?

Jerome   Things over and done with. Things that would hurt you. Things that it's hard to believe I ever did now.

Penny (*beat*)   Women?

Jerome   One woman.

Penny (*beat*)   These last few months . . . Did I know her?

Jerome   You didn't know me.

Penny   Me lying awake . . . worried that you were working too hard. (*Beat, quietly.*) Bastard.

Jerome   Yes.

Penny   Sick bastard. (*Unable to control her temper.*) Who was she? I'm no fool, I saw signs, had suspicions . . . I even asked Clara to keep an eye out for me in work . . . long lunch breaks, clients asking for you especially.

Jerome   What did Clara say?

Penny   That you didn't have it in you to cheat anyone. I felt like a neurotic housewife . . . my life so dull I had to imagine things.

Jerome   You like Clara, don't you?

Penny   At parties women say – the condescending bitches – that I'm so lucky to paint full-time at home. Then they switch off, like my thoughts couldn't interest them. She's a boring housewife, they think, tarted up under a new name. I gave up a career in RTE for us, for our child . . . I never went back because I'd hoped that in six months or a year we'd start all over . . . (*Stops.*) Clara listens at least, makes me feel like an intelligent human being.

Jerome   Penny . . . I'm sorry.

Gradually what he means dawns on her.

Penny (*softly*)   Oh my God . . .

She sinks on to the bed, her shoulders hunched. Awkwardly **Jerome**
tries to approach, his hand out.

Penny (*quietly*)   Don't you touch . . . never, ever touch . . .

Jerome   I knew it was wrong, utterly, breathtakingly wrong.
I did it to feel wrong, to at least feel something. I don't even
know who I was trying to punish.

Penny   I don't want to know.

Jerome   Spite at myself, spite at you for putting up with me.
Spite at life for cheating me. Always trying to compensate,
trying to be someone else, someone different, trying to fuck
my way back into feeling something even if it was wrong.

Penny   I said I don't want to know.

Jerome   Clara genuinely liked you.

Penny (*rises in fury*)   Stop it! You cunt! You pox-ridden self-
righteous jumped-up cock-sucking little Papist Carlow
bogman prick. Stop it or I'll drill holes in parts of you that
Christ never even dreamt of!

Jerome   I don't expect forgiveness.

Penny   It's myself I can't forgive for being so stupid. That's
why you wanted the use of this flat, isn't it?

Jerome   Partly. Yes.

Penny   You pair deserve each other.

Jerome   It's finished.

Penny   Not for my sake, I hope. I don't want you back. Me
arriving here like a fool, thinking this might finally be about
healing. (*Colder.*) This is between your over-sized middle-aged
conscience and your under-sized middle-aged prick. Maybe
Clara might take you back till she gets bored of her conquest.
But there are junkies in these flats with more self-respect than
you. Your mother always thought you were God anyway, now
you're just modelling the uniform. You've no home left and
you'll find no friends either, because your friends are as

shallow as sound bites and you'll just make them nervous. You'll rot in this stinking room and nobody will care. Not Clara and not me, because you've killed any feelings I ever had.

Jerome   I never wanted to hurt you.

Penny   Then why did you have to tell me?

Jerome   So that you'd turn against me. I don't know what these wounds are leading up to. If anything happens to me I don't want you regretting my absence.

Penny (*drained*)   Just let me go now. Please. I can't bear looking at you.

Jerome   I'll cover my hands . . .

Penny   It's your eyes. I fell in love with them the first time we met. So unnaturally bright. Stop looking at me with them. You're too much like the man I fell in love with. He died seven years ago and there's no resurrection from the dead. When you fucked Clara you fucked away whatever was left of my dreams. Who gets to keep our solicitor?

Jerome   Take everything. I won't contest it.

Penny   What's left to take? Bricks and mortar as barren as you left me.

Jerome   Don't say that.

Penny   It's you who wanted to speak the truth. I loved you with all my heart till you smashed it.

Jerome   I had to tell you. You're a part of me and I couldn't keep lying to my own soul.

Penny (*quietly*)   Send someone over for your clothes, please. I couldn't bear having to look at you again.

She exits without looking back. **Jerome** *sits with his head in his hands as lights fade.*

Scene Seven

The blackout is disturbed by the noise of boxes falling. Sufficient light bleeds in to reveal **Jerome** *sitting up in bed, startled. He is naked except for a pair of underpants. Another box falls with a loud crash. From nowhere a cup hurtles across the stage and smashes.* **Jerome** *switches on the bedside lamp.*

Jerome (*trying to control his fear*)   Is that you, boy? (*There's another bang. He rises.*) I'm not afraid, I don't know what you want.

First Thug*'s voice* (*mockingly ghostly*)   A blow job!

Jerome *turns in terror to be confronted by three thugs (who may wear balaclavas if played by actors in overlapping roles). They rise, convulsed with laughter, from behind the boxes.*

Third Thug (*slurred, almost retarded tone*)   Dick head.

Jerome (*summoning courage*)   What do you want here?

First Thug   We came to see the freak show.

Second Thug   Where are you bleeding from, pal? I'm from bleeding Ballybough meself!

The others crack up at the joke, as all three advance menacingly, boxing him in.

Jerome   I want you out of here. This is my flat.

Third Thug   Dick head!

Jerome   What time is it?

First Thug (*recites like a sinister nursery rhyme*)   One o'clock, two o'clock, three o'clock, four: Look who just walked through your door.

Jerome   You're trespassing.

First Thug   Wrong, pal! You're the geezer who doesn't belong. I hear you want to save us, the binmen will be hauling away sacks of crutches. Nobody will be able to use their disability passes when you're finished with us, no more bleeding free travel or medical cards.

Second Thug   You tell the bollix, Joey.

Third Thug   Dick head!

First Thug   You never stop to think that maybe we don't fucking want you, pal? Up here crucifying yourself. We'd have done it for you, nailed you to the fucking floor if you wanted.

Second Thug   Give the spacer a kicking and let's get the fuck out of here.

Third Thug   Dick head's got it coming!

First Thug   Naw, he'd enjoy that too much. Dick head obviously likes pain. You know what we'll do, lads? Tie him to the bleeding table, rip the knicks off him, loosen him up with a big tub of axle grease and then leave him there . . . do nothing. (*The others chuckle menacingly.*) His disappointment would only be fierce. I mean what sort of weirdo punches holes in his fucking hands. (*He suddenly grabs* **Jerome** *by the hair.*) That's what you did, pal, wasn't it? Wasn't it?

Jerome   No.

First Thug   No, me bollix. You can spin fairy stories for little old ladies, like Mrs Boyle whose granddaughter is dying. Get their hopes up, eh? But we're men of the world, no arseing around with us. (*He grabs* **Jerome***'s hair even tighter.*) So fucking admit it.

Jerome (*wincing in pain*)   This was God's will.

First Thug (*punching him in the stomach*)   Don't mess with us, pal! Barrelling in from your posh suburb. I'll not have it, you understand?

He punches **Jerome** *again and lets him fall to his knees, clutching his stomach.*

First Thug   It's time you copped on that people don't like being taken for mugs.

Jerome   I only came here for a screw, a quiet bit on the side, you understand?

Third Thug   Horny old Dick head.

First Thug   That's more like it. Did she use her stilettos?

Jerome   Mock all you wish. But there's a child's soul trapped here.

First Thug   I believe this, pal. You're a looper, spouting horse-shit and expecting me to swallow it.

Second Thug   Make him squeal like a pig, Joey.

First Thug (*to* **Second Thug**)   Shut the fuck up, you! (*To* **Jerome**.) What else did Jesus tell you? Did he give you tablets of stone we can wrap them around your neck before fucking you down the lift-shaft?

Jerome   My watch, it cost five hundred quid, (*He removes his watch.*) you'll get money for it. Take it, please just leave me alone.

First Thug   Giz a look. (*He examines the watch, then throws it to the* **Third Thug**.) You were robbed, pal. A piece of shit. Don't worry, we'll clean you out all right, you're asking for it. But let's have our bit of fun first. You see I heard them talk about you in the pub and you got my goat, because I hate Jesus merchants, especially when they prick around with old ladies. So says I to myself, this fecker needs bringing down a peg or two.

He suddenly kicks **Jerome** *in the stomach.* **Jerome** *curls up into a ball, moaning on the floor.*

First Thug   You insult my intelligence, pal, so give up this charade, right!

Jerome *struggles back to his knees, glancing around into the empty spaces.*

Jerome   He's here. Now.

First Thug   Who?

Jerome   The boy, his spirit.

Second Thug *and* **Third Thug** *look around uneasily.*

First Thug   Don't mess with me, it's dangerous. (*He slips behind* **Jerome** *and grabs his hair, jerking his head back.*) Repeat after me, 'I am a total fraud . . .'

Jerome   Our father who art in heaven . . .

First Thug (*tightening grip*)   You're no listening, pal.

Jerome (*going into a world of his own*)   Hallowed be Thy name . . .

First Thug (*enraged, pulling his hair*)   'I am a total fraud' . . . say it, you cunt! Don't pretend you're not scared of me. You're scared, chicken-shit scared!

Jerome *kneels, trance-like, overawed by the words spilling from him in a child's scared voice, seemingly oblivious to the thugs surrounding him.*

Jerome   Scared, yes, so scared. So alone, here, always alone, no one to share this pain, no one to hear. Daddy dead in the bed, eyes wide, vomit on his lips. Left me here, scared, alone. Don't want to be left alone, yet don't know how to leave, where to go. I'm scared . . . light in the distance down a black tunnel. I can see it but not reach. Faces beckoning I cannot touch. Warmth, so close to that warmth, but keep getting jerked back by this rope, this knot around my neck, so tight, trapped. Cut me down, someone please cut me down . . . help me, release me, share this pain.

The **Second Thug** *has moved behind the* **First Thug**, *while the* **Third Thug** *steps in front of* **Jerome**, *whose words unnerve them all.*

First Thug (*to* **Third Thug**)   Give him a boot in the bollix, burst his guts open, you hear me!

Jerome   I want my mother, want my father . . . want us to be happy, I want the shouting to stop, the drinking. Want to stop pissing the bed, want him not to hit her, no more screaming, no more . . . All gone, gone. Don't want to be left alone, like all the other times, all the others who left, the lights out and everything dark, just rats scurrying beneath my feet that almost touch the floor. I want the little Galway girl to come back, to play on the floor where I played, I want to touch the toys in her cot at night, lean over her when she sleeps. And all the others who ran away. I want someone to stay. I want someone to see me. Here. Why can you not see me hanging here? Not see that I'm in pain, not cut the rope from around my neck? I want somebody to play Jesus for me, to suffer, to die, to rise again, to bring me with him. Take me to Jesus, take me past the faces, down the tunnel into the blazing light.

During this speech the **Second Thug** *finds that his body begins to silently buckle forward. It leans so much over to one side that he almost seems to be defying gravity. It seems impossible he can stay standing. The others do not notice him.*

First Thug (*freaked*)   Shut this fucker up!

The **Third Thug** *goes to kick* **Jerome** *as the* **First Thug** *still holds* **Jerome**'s *hair, but something in the* **First Thug**'s *face stops him.*

First Thug   Shift your hand from my shoulder, Tommo.

Second Thug (*terrified whisper*)   Joey, I'm not bleeding near you. Joey? Look, Joey.

Jerome   I want the doors and the window to open. I want the roof torn off. I'd fly if you'd only cut the rope from my neck.

First Thug (*hint of terror*)   Quit fucking messing, Tommo, shift your hand from my neck. It's like ice.

He puts his other hand on his shoulder, feeling something and buckles slightly forward in terror.

Jerome   I want someone to take away my pain, to let it flow freely through them like blood from a wound.

Second Thug (*freaked whisper*)   Joey, Joey, what the fuck's happening, Joey?

Jerome   Just stand beside me, put your arms around me and lift my body down. I'm so scared to face God, his light pulsating, beckoning. His heat, a white flame. I've been cold for too long. Let me pass through your body, your arteries, your veins, let me flow inside your blood, let me be redeemed.

The **First Thug** *slowly lets go of* **Jerome**'s *hair. He turns his head to the left, gripped by terror, his body starting to mimic the same mimed contortions as that of the* **Second Thug***. They watch each other in silent horror, while* **Jerome**'s *own body jerks and buckles, his hands stretching outwards. The contortions begin to spread into the* **Third Thug**'s *body as well. They seem trapped, no longer in control of their own bodies.*

Jerome (*own voice*)   Jesus, I feel him like ice into steam, wings into flight. Go, for Christ's sake, go. Lord, cast his soul to heaven or hell, but take his soul from here.

The boxes in the corner suddenly collapse. The **First Thug** *screams and falls over as if whatever force was holding up upright has suddenly let go. He freaks his companions who fall likewise. The* **First Thug** *staggers to his feet and runs for the exit, followed by the* **Second Thug***. The* **Third Thug** *manages to launch one huge kick at* **Jerome**'s *stomach before following them.*

Third Thug (*screaming in terror*)   Dick head!

He exits and **Jerome** *lies alone, curled up in pain as the lights fade.*

Scene Eight

Lights rise, suggesting morning. **Jerome** *lies in the same spot, in his underpants. His nose is blooded. He looks dazed, half-dead as* **Rita** *enters and stops.*

Rita   Mister, are you all right, Mister?

Jerome (*getting to his knees slowly*)   An accident. I must have fallen.

Rita   I came to tell you . . .

Jerome (*pulling a quilt around his shoulders*)   I'm sorry about what happened in the hospital. Now leave me alone, please . . .

Rita   It's about my granddaughter.

Jerome   I can't help her or anyone.

Rita   She died . . . just after four a.m. this morning.

Jerome (*turns slowly*)   I'm sorry. I couldn't prevent it, anymore than with my own child.

Rita   I know.

Jerome   There's nothing I can do for you.

Rita   You've done enough already.

Jerome   Don't mock me or take pity . . . Some quirk made my hands blister. They've stopped bleeding now.

Rita   You're a good man.

Jerome   I've done nothing in life that wasn't motivated by self-interest. But believe me, if I could have taken your granddaughter's place I would.

Rita   We all would have. Me, my daughter, the girl's father. We'd have gladly died to let her live on. But we couldn't, for all the longing inside us.

Jerome   You shouldn't have come here. You should be with people you know, who can give you comfort.

Rita   No one can give me comfort . . . not ever . . . only courage. Little Jacinta had more courage in her skinny body than this whole city put together. She woke . . . I didn't know what time of night it was, her mother and I had dozed off beside the bed. Her eyes seemed to wake me, so blue. (*A child's voice.*) 'I saw a man, Gran. I had a dream. The carriageway down to the library was empty. The roundabout empty, everywhere empty. And this lovely piebald horse came galloping down from the standing stones on the slope. Galloping towards me, with great friendly eyes. And he was up on it, Gran, some man with blood soaking from his hands. "It's all right, Jacinta," he says, "you can let go now, your Mam will be okay and your Gran too without you. It's all right to let go this pain if you want." Then he disappeared, but he left the big piebald horse there . . . waiting for me to climb up on its back.' (*Own voice.*) I looked at my daughter, I knew she couldn't speak. 'If that's what you want, Jessie,' I told her. 'We'll be fine, you climb up whenever you want.' She closed her eyes, settling back into sleep, but I knew she was dying. And we just sat with her, surrounded by all those drips and monitors. We didn't even phone her father. Somehow he knew to come in. I'd forgotten what Jacinta looked like when not in pain. Yet I never saw her as content, that blip, blip, blip on the machine till it stopped.

Jerome (*long beat*)　I did nothing. It was just a dream. Who knows what drugs she was on.

Rita　Maybe so. Or maybe not.

Jerome　Will you be all right?

Rita　She's waiting for me, at the end of time. (*Beat.*) How sore are your hands?

Jerome　You can only just see the scars now.

Rita　I was angry with you and with life yesterday. I felt cheated by God. I said things to people, called you names. I had a rage burning inside me that needed to get out.

Jerome　Nobody said anything to me.

Rita　Are you sure? What happened here?

Jerome　I fell over . . . stupidly drinking.

Rita　Will you stay here?

Jerome　It's my brother's flat. He's coming home with his girlfriend and kids.

Rita　You'll go back home so?

Jerome　I don't know where I can go.

Rita　I'll think of you . . . some nights when I wake.

Jerome　I'll think of you.

Rita   Think of wee Jacinta too.

She turns to exit and meets **Derek** *coming in the doorway. They exchange a look and pass.* **Derek** *stands, surveying* **Jerome**.

Derek   Who the hell was that?

Jerome   Just a neighbour. You're back?

Derek   It didn't work out.

Jerome *reaches for his clothes and quickly begins to dress as he talks.*

Jerome   You tried at least.

Derek   I thought you were going to paint the place.

Jerome   I was clearing things out, getting it ready. Catherine's kids, they must be tired.

Derek   She's paying off the taxi down below. We won't stay here for long.

Jerome   It's a home for you, a start, you're lucky.

Derek   Don't mock.

Jerome   I'd swap with you if I could.

Derek   Sure. I'll call you in work.

Jerome   I won't be there.

Derek   At home so.

Jerome   Not there either. Not unless one day . . .

Derek   What's going on?

Jerome   I don't know. I should feel scared. But there's a presence, beating within the beat of my own heart. I'd forgotten that it used to be there when I was a child. I don't deserve to feel it, a puny scared-shitless nobody like me. (*He puts on his jacket.*) By the way, neighbours may try to scare you off with stories. Ignore them, there's nothing here now. Here . . . (*He reaches into his pocket and produces a few crumpled notes.*) it's not much, but get something for the two little girls.

Derek (*confused, concerned*)   Where are you going, brother?

Jerome   To start again as myself.

He exits with **Derek** *looking after him puzzled as the lights go down.*
End.

Note to directors/designers

The dilemma for any designer is to create an intensely claustrophobic atmosphere within the flat itself (with a slightly raked floor), while allowing sufficient flexibility for parts of the stage to convey other locations uncluttered by more than the most basic props when required.

This may be achieved by flying in basic props from above, by the use of silent black-clad dressers working with swift but unhurried movements to move props on-stage, or by whatever other device is appropriate to the logic of individual productions.

Although for the creation of a physical haunting tension within the flat a certain element of realism is necessary, it is still preferable that props and trickery be kept to a minimum (although vital that certain objects appear to move by themselves). Mime and movement may prove better vehicles than complex pyrotechnics to create a sense of actual haunting on stage.

Printed in the USA
CPSIA information can be obtained
at www.ICGtesting.com
LVHW041059171024
794057LV00001B/166

9 780413 738806